It's Your Law

It's Your Law

By CHARLES P. CURTIS

Harvard University Press, Cambridge

1954

Copyright, 1954

By the President and Fellows of Harvard College

Distributed in Great Britain by
GEOFFREY CUMBERLEGE
Oxford University Press
London

The selections from Alfred North Whitehead, *Modes of Thought* (Copyright, 1938, by The Macmillan Company), and from Alfred North Whitehead, *Adventures of Ideas* (Copyright, 1933, by The Macmillan Company) are used with the publishers' permission.

Library of Congress Catalog Card Number 54-9773

Printed in the United States of America

To
FRANCES

I have written lovingly about the Law. Unless I loved it, I could not hope to understand it. And I have written candidly, because otherwise you would not want to read what I write. Moreover, there are people to whom it is as foolish as it is false to be less than candid, just as there are others to whom candor is simply offensive.

I have tried to write about the most interesting things in the Law, because I think they are most likely to be the important things.

C. P. C.

CONTENTS

The Advocate

The Adversary Process

Justice is a chilly virtue. It is of high importance that we be introduced into the inhospitable halls of justice by a friend. I think we neglect the fact that the first function of the lawyer, and the first great purpose of the devotion which a lawyer owes to his client, is the overcoming of this feeling of unfriendliness. The first duty of the bar is to make sure that everyone who feels the need of a friend in court shall have one, and I am not talking only of the poor and indigent. They obviously need a friend, and a good judge will fill the need if the bar does not. Nor only of those whose cause we detest. A proper sense of advocacy will take care of them, and I will speak of that in its place. I mean everyone, including those who seem least to need a friend, those who have the most respect for the law and who are usually the least familiar with it and the most fearful.

But if the devotion a lawyer owes to his client were no more than friendliness, if it were simply to serve the purpose of taking the chill off justice, there would be no more to say. We make greater demands upon our lawyers than that. They must be not only our friends. They must be our champions. For the way we administer justice is by an adversary proceeding, which is as much as to say, we set the parties fighting. This has been so for some time; in fact, according to Max Radin, since about the fourth or the fifth century B.C. in Rome, when, Radin says, the judge's task changed from determining the truth to the umpiring of a competition. "At a certain special stage in the history of Western society," Radin said, "the way in which it was done was to call upon the judge to umpire a contest. His task was not to determine truth, but to decide who had the best of a competition—a competition that was not originally one of argument, though it soon became one. The place and time of this event can be set with fair probability at Rome somewhere in the fifth or fourth centuries B.C. . . For many modern lawyers it is difficult to conceive of a trial as anything else, although the words 'trial' and 'verdict' might have called attention to the fact that these things professed to be something quite different." [1]

This is still largely true. There is the story of the two prizefighters, who had been witnesses in a case and went in and stood in the back of the courtroom where Chief Justice Lemuel Shaw was presiding, as great a judge as his son-in-law, Herman Melville, was a writer. Two blue-black jaws dropped in admiration, and one said, not so much to the other as to himself, "Christ, what a referee!"

Lemuel Shaw was the Chief Justice of Massachusetts a hundred years ago—not so very long in the life of the law—but only a few years ago Mr. Justice Jackson of the United States Supreme Court said, in an opinion on the right of one lawyer to force his opponent to disclose some papers, "A common law trial is and always should be an adversary proceeding." [2] And in the course of a discussion of Trial Tactics sponsored by the American Bar Association in 1951, Lon Hocker of St. Louis, a distinguished trial lawyer, followed this by adding, "If there is any message which I can leave with a younger trial lawyer, this is the one I yearn most to impart: the trial of a lawsuit is an adversary business." [3] I'll quote Mr. Hocker again later.

I find it quite impossible to understand trial by ordeal, where justice apparently used to be put to the touch of a small miracle, but anyone who has been anywhere near a piece of determined litigation will readily understand trial by battle.

"One other method of proof was one introduced into England by the Normans, and this was trial by battle. In civil cases it was not fought between the parties themselves, but between their respective champions. . . We very soon find from the rolls that there was a professional band of champions who undertook business all over the country; courts would arrange the dates of battle so that the champions could fit in their engagements conveniently. Some very great landowners, such as the larger monasteries, were so constantly involved in litigation that they maintained their own full-time champions. But in criminal cases battle was a much more serious affair. It lay when a private person brought a criminal charge against another, and was fought by the accuser and accused in person. It was deadly; if the defeated defendant was not already slain in the battle he was immediately hanged on the gallows which stood ready." [4]

There are some subjects of litigation in which the adversary proceeding is an admirable way of administering justice. One wise judge implied as much when Charles E. Wyzanski said, "A political libel suit is the modern substitute for ordeal by battle. It is the means which society has chosen to induce bitter partisans to wager money instead of exchanging bloody noses." [5] But litigation by an adversary proceeding is the way we cut the knot of many disputes in which it is disastrously inappropriate. Divorces, the custody of children, will contests, almost any kind of dispute which springs from family or equally intimate dissension—there a broken bone is more easily mendable. And it is intolerably too often true that a criminal trial turns into an adversary proceeding. "Criminal justice is concerned with the pathology of the body politic. In administering the criminal law, judges wield the most awesome surgical instruments of society. A criminal trial, it has been well said, should have the atmosphere of the operating room. The presiding judge determines the atmosphere. He is not an umpire who enforces the rules of a game, or merely a moderator between contestants. If he is adequate to his functions, the moral authority which he radiates will impose the indispensable standards of dignity and austerity upon all those who participate in a criminal trial." [6]

What, then, is the justification for this approach to justice, other than the fact we are several centuries used to it and aside from the fact that spectators in small communities and newspaper readers in cities enjoy the spectacle? It seems to me that the justification of the adversary proceeding is the satisfaction of the parties, and not our satisfaction, except as we too are prospective litigants. This is a rational justification of the adversary approach to justice. Along this line, what the law is trying to do is give the algebraic maximum of satisfaction to both parties. This is a crude, but indeed it is not a bad, definition of the justice which the adversary proceeding provides. The law is trying to do justice between the parties for the parties rather than for us, trying to give them their own justice so far as possible and so far as compatible with what may be distinguished as our justice.

It is necessary, to be sure, to apply the general terms of what we regard as justice to their particular case. For we too must be satisfied. We are prospective customers. But the difference is not great. They are some of us, and they are much influenced by what we regard as just. The law pays more attention to the satisfaction of the needs of the parties in the particular case than it does to our ideas about justice in general. The law takes the position that we ought to be satisfied if the parties are; and it believes that the best way to get that done is to encourage them to fight it out, and dissolve their differences in dissension. We are still a combative people, not yet so civilized and sophisticated as to forget that combat is one way to justice.

We even try to delude ourselves into thinking that combat is the best way. The fact is, the adversary process is an indispensable alternative to the best way to what we may hope to be a wise as well as a just decision. I mean a few candid people pooling their minds on a problem, and not so much arguing with each other as eliciting each other's arguments.

I am afraid this is too flattering a description of our other way to justice, that parties settle their disputes privately and at their own expense; and yet there is a great deal to be said for settlement as a way of administering the law, granted, of course, that a judgment after a trial is a constant alternative. It might even be said that one of the great functions of our courts is to be just that, no more than a constant alternative, to make it certain that the discount in the discounted law which is applied in settlements shall be figured on true value and not on some arbitrary sum. Certainly a great many more cases are settled than tried. No one knows how many because there is no way of defining a case that has not been brought.

Negotiations for settlement are themselves judicial proceedings. Each attorney sits in judgment on the contentions of the other, comparing them with his own prophecies of what a judge would do, as the judge in turn would prophesy what the court of appeal will do. The evidence consists in the claims of each attorney discounted to the prophecy of the other. The negotiations are, indeed, the proceedings of a court of preliminary instance; and they have the virtue of being conducted in private, with each party less committed to his own contentions, and less embittered by the other's. A settlement ends, if it is successful, in a compromise instead of a judgment. Compromise is as often the better part of justice as prudence is the better part of valor, more often than we who are used to the adversary processing of justice are likely to think. But your lawyer is no less your champion in a settlement out of court than he is your champion in the battle in court.

The devotion and the fidelity which a lawyer owes to his client is great enough to strew quandaries and perplexities in the way of his relations with his clients which seem to me to be peculiar to his profession. At any rate, these perplexities offer us by far the best, indeed so far as I know, the only approach to some understanding of the chief function of the lawyer in the law, which is advocacy. And the heart of advocacy, as with other things of the spirit, lies in its ethics.

A Lawyer's Loyalties

I want first of all to put advocacy in its proper setting. It is a special case of vicarious conduct. A lawyer devotes his life and career to acting for other people. So too do the parson and the priest, and, in another way, the banker. The banker handles other people's money. The parson and the priest handle other people's spiritual aspirations. A lawyer handles other people's troubles.

But there is a difference. The loyalty of a clergyman runs, not to the particular parishioner whose joys or troubles he is busy with, but to his church; and the banker looks to his bank. It is the church or the bank on whose behalf they are acting, which serves the communicant or the borrower. Thus their loyalties run in a different direction from a lawyer's.

So too when a lawyer works for the government, his loyalties, like the clergyman's, hang on a superior peg. It is fiction to say that he has the government for his client. The government is too big. It absorbs him. He is a part of it.

Likewise the general counsel for a corporation. His identification with his client is all but complete. Taft, in some lectures at the Albany Law School,[7] referring to work in the legal department of a corporation, said, "Such employment leads to a lawyer's becoming nothing more than an officer of the corporation as closely identified with it as if he was the president, the secretary or the treasurer."[8] Indeed, he usually is a director or a vice-president.

Not so the lawyer in private practice. His loyalty runs to his client. Not the court? you ask. Does not the court take the same position as the church or the bank? Is not the lawyer an officer of the court? Why doesn't the court have first claim on his loyalty? No, in a paradoxical way. The lawyer's official duty, required of him indeed by the court, is to devote himself to the client. He has two masters, and it is sometimes hard to say which comes first. There are occasions when our system of justice seems to give the nod to the client.

Lord Brougham, in his defense of Queen Caroline in her divorce case, told the House of Lords, "I once before took occasion to remind your Lordships, which was unnecessary, but there are many whom it may be needful to remind, that an advocate, by the sacred duty which he owes his client, knows in the discharge of that office but one person in the world—that client and no other. . . Nay, separating even the duties of a patriot from those of an advocate, and casting them if need be to the wind, he must go on reckless of the consequences, if his fate it should unhappily be to involve his country in confusion for his client's protection."[9]

Lord Brougham was a great advocate, and when he made this statement he was arguing a great case, the divorce of Queen Caroline from George IV before the House of Lords. Plainly he was exerting more than his learning and more than his legal ability. Years later he explained this to William Forsyth, the author of a book on lawyers called *Hortensius,* who had asked him what he meant. Before you read Brougham's reply, let me remind you that the king, George IV, was the one who was pressing the divorce which Brougham was defending, and that George had contracted a secret marriage, while he was heir apparent, with Mrs. Fitzherbert, a Roman Catholic. Brougham knew this, and knew too that it was enough to deprive the king of his crown under the Act of Settlement. Brougham wrote:

"The real truth is, that the statement was anything rather than a deliberate and well-considered opinion. It was a menace, and it was addressed chiefly to George IV, but also to wiser men, such as Castlereagh and Wellington. I was prepared, *in case of necessity,* that is, in case the Bill passed the Lords, to do two things—first, to resist it in the Commons *with the country at my back*; but next, if need be, to dispute the King's title, to show he had forfeited the crown by marrying a Catholic, in the words of the Act, 'as if he were naturally dead.' What I said was fully understood by Geo. IV; perhaps by the Duke of Castlereagh, and I am confident it would have prevented them from pressing the Bill beyond a certain point." [10]

Lord Brougham's menace has become the classic statement of the loyalty which a lawyer owes to his client, perhaps because, being a menace, it is so extreme. And yet the Canons of Ethics of the American Bar Association are scarcely more moderate. "The lawyer owes 'entire devotion to the interest of the client, warm zeal in the maintenance and defense of his rights and the exertion of his utmost learning and ability,' to the end that nothing be taken or be withheld from him, save by the rules of law, legally applied." [11]

How entire is this devotion and how warm is this zeal? How much *alter* do they together put in the lawyer's *ego*? How far from himself do they draw a lawyer? How much less than himself, as a patriot and a citizen and an individual, do they require a lawyer to be? These are hard questions, as hard to ask as I think they are hard to answer.

The Canon has no difficulty with its answer, "But it is steadfastly to be borne in mind that the great trust of a lawyer is to be performed within and not without the bounds of the law. The office of attorney does not permit, much less does it demand of him for any client, violation of law or any manner of fraud or chicane. He must obey his own conscience and not that of his client."

That's all very well and easily said, but acting for others is in a different category of behavior than acting for yourself and I think its ethics are different. Let me examine this proposition with some care and in some detail.

The person for whom you are acting very reasonably expects you to treat him better than you do other people, which is just another way of saying that you owe him a higher standard of conduct than you owe to others. This goes back a long way. It is the pre-platonic ethics which Socrates disposed of at the very outset of the *Republic*; that is, that justice consists of doing good to your friends and harm to your enemies. A lawyer, therefore, insensibly finds himself treating his client better than others; and therefore others worse than his client. A lawyer, or a trustee, or anyone acting for another, has lower standards of conduct toward outsiders than he has toward his clients or his beneficiaries against the outsiders. He is required to treat outsiders as if they were barbarians and enemies. The more devotion and zeal the lawyer owes to his client, the less he owes to others when he is acting for his client. It is as if a man had only so much virtue, and the more he gives to one, the less he has available for anyone else. The upshot is that a man whose business it is to act for others finds himself, in his dealings on his client's behalf with outsiders, acting on a lower standard than he would if he were acting for himself, lower than any standard his client himself would be willing to act on, lower in fact than anyone on his own.

You devote yourself to the interests of another at the peril of yourself. Vicarious action tempts a man away from himself. Men will do for others what they are not willing to do for themselves—nobler as well as ignoble things. What I want to do now is to illustrate this in the practice of law by a number of perplexing situations. They raise ethical problems, but none of them, I think, has a simple right or wrong answer, and I know of no canons of ethics or morals which lead to any answer. How could there be when they ignore the cause of the perplexity, which is the difference between acting for another and acting for yourself?

I will give you a personal case. I was a trustee under a will. My co-trustee was away, and had left me with the duty of trying to sell a piece of real estate. I got an offer of $50,000 which I agreed orally to accept. They left to draw up the agreement for me to sign, but before they had it ready I received a cash offer of $55,000. So I was on the spot, for under the Statute of Frauds, as any lawyer knows, I was not legally bound on an oral contract to sell real estate.

I didn't know quite what to do. I called up the purchaser and the broker and told them to bring their lawyer with them. And I said to them, "I have received an offer of $55,000, and either you are going to make me an offer of $55,000 cash or I am going to take up that offer and go back on my word, which I gave you. Unless you," then I turned to the lawyer, "can show me out of the correspondence that I am bound under the Statute of Frauds." By way of peroration I added, "If you want to call me a son of a bitch, do, because I am going to do just that, and I heartily agree that I am a son of a bitch to do it."

I didn't like it. They were very angry. Their lawyer was no help. He had the correspondence, but he didn't point to anything I had written which legally bound me.

I went back to my office, turned my file over to one of my partners, and said, "Am I bound under the statute?" My partner took the file, came back the next day, and to my great relief, he had spelled enough out of the correspondence to convince me that I was bound. I called up the lawyer and laughed at him somewhat, and everyone was happy; except that no one complimented me and no one expressed any disagreement with what I had called myself.

I did not enjoy the situation, but I was confident that I had done right. Years later Professor Austin W. Scott, who has written the one and only best book on trusts and trustees, told me there was an English case I ought to read. It was not so long ago—1950—in London. Mrs. Simpson—not the one you think—rented a house in London and decided she wanted to buy it. She offered the owners, who were three trustees, 6,000 pounds, and they agreed. All the terms of the sale were agreed to, except who should pay the expenses of the sale, which amounted to 142 pounds. At that point, one of the several beneficiaries of the trust, a Canon Buttle, also offered 6,000 pounds. Mrs. Simpson then agreed to pay the expenses. This made hers the better offer, and a contract of sale was drawn up, signed by Mrs. Simpson, and signed by one, only one, of the three trustees. Canon Buttle promptly offered 6,500 pounds, which made his the better offer. The trustees informed the canon that they felt that the sale to Mrs. Simpson could not properly be cancelled and Canon Buttle brought suit against them, to require them to sell the property to him for 6,500 pounds, substantially more than the 6,142 pounds which was Mrs. Simpson's offer.

Was the canon right? This is what Judge Wynn-Parry said. "The trustees felt in a position of great embarrassment. They felt in honour bound to proceed with the proposed sale to Mrs. Simpson. . . They felt that all considerations of commercial morality required that they should proceed with the contract." Let me interrupt to remind you that two of the three trustees had not signed it and that it had not yet been delivered to the lady. The judge went on, "My view is that the trustees and their solicitors acted on an incorrect principle. The only consideration which was present to their minds was that they had gone so far in the negotiations with Mrs. Simpson that they could not properly, from the point of view of commercial morality, resile from those negotiations."

Fortunately, these sad stories usually have a happier ending than you expect. Mrs. Simpson raised her offer to 6,600 pounds, and everyone, including Canon Buttle, felt better. It would have been interesting to have sat in on the conversations which we may suppose were held between the good canon and the solicitors for the trustees, while the churchman argued for the strict law and the lawyers argued for the principles of morality.[12] But the law was against the lawyers and against the conscience of the trustees, as it was against mine.

The ethical problems of a lawyer are not so simple as the canon, either canon for that matter, thinks.

Duties and Dangers in Advocacy

I will give you an extreme case, for an extreme case is the best test of a hard problem. May it ever become the duty of a lawyer to tell a lie for his client? Does a lawyer's duty to his client, the duty which is enjoined upon him by law and by the obligations of his profession, include telling a lie in his client's behalf?

On my answer to this question, I have had critical help. Some of it came from lawyers who angrily denied that a lawyer should ever tell a lie. Their angry denials shed a somewhat lurid light on the problem, but it was helpful for it made me reconsider my answer. Less lurid and more illuminating criticism came from the more reasoned denials, but the most illumination came from those who knew there was a problem and recognized its difficulties. I have profited by all these criticisms, but my answer remains the same as what I wrote in 1951 in the article in the *Stanford Law Review* which brought them to me.[13] They have led me to clarify some ambiguities and correct some misstatements, but they have not changed my conclusion that the problem exists and that there are occasions when it does become a lawyer's duty to lie for his client, rare as they are, in this extreme case of his devotion to his client.

Perhaps I have done wrong to use the word, lie. I wish I could think of a better word. There are devout theologians who understand what I mean as mental reservations or restrictions, but I am not talking to them, nor do I need to. They know that the Eighth Commandment enjoins more than veracity and that we can be false in our relations to others as well as false in our relation to the truth, as we see it. The only objection to the word, lie, is that it has only three letters, one less, and so the more offensive, than those ugly four-letter words. I am sorry if it gives offense, but I can think of no other which fits the extreme case I am going to talk about.

At the other extreme stands candor. A lawyer whose conscience required him to be as candid and ingenuous for his clients in his practice as he was for himself would be disbarred almost before he knew it. And quite rightly, for he would be betraying his clients and if all lawyers were equally candid, it would make an end of our adversary system of justice.

Suppose, at a pretrial hearing, the judge should ask one of the lawyers if he had authority to settle the case for any less than what he had just demanded and the other lawyer had refused. Certainly the judge had no right to ask such an unconscionable question, but we are supposing he did. Does the lawyer simply decline to answer? His client had authorized him to settle for substantially less, but only if his lawyer thought he could not get more. The lawyer thought he could get more and that was what he was trying to do.

If he simply declines to answer, isn't he in effect by clear implication, telling the other lawyer that he would take less if he can't get more, and thus put it out of his power to get any more? And note that what this unhappy, and angry, lawyer would be telling his opponent by declining to answer the judge was not true until he declined to answer. Until then he had no authority to settle for less because he thought he could get more. He made it true by declining to answer.

I suggest that our lawyer would do better by answering the judge with a flat denial, "No, that is the least I am authorized to settle for." This would be something less than candid, but it would be the truth so long as he thought he could get it, for his client authorized him to settle for less only if he thought he couldn't. It would be a true statement, but not a true answer to the judge's question, for he was assuming that the other lawyer wasn't going to pay more. What a tangled web we weave, when we find we must deceive!

What does the poor lawyer do then? He goes right to the judge's chambers without the other lawyer, insists on seeing him alone, and explains. This may be hard to do, unless the judge has had a twist of conscience. Otherwise our lawyer goes to another judge, and relieves his conscience without betraying his client.

Let me tell you the story of Sam the Lookout as a parable. It was told to me as a true story, but that does not make it any the less good as a parable. I know no relation more like the relation between a lawyer and his client than that between a seaman, captain or sailor, and his ship. Sit in with a distinguished New York lawyer who was once called over to a conference of admiralty lawyers with the crew of a ship which had been in a collision. The lawyers were going over the testimony which the members of the crew would give at the approaching trial. Finally they came to Sam, the lookout, and the Captain, who was asking the questions, turned to him and said, "You, of course, were up in the eyes on the forecastle keeping a sharp lookout." The seaman squirmed in his chair, twisted his cap, and said, "The truth is, Captain, I was in the head having a smoke." The lawyers leaned forward, but the Captain turned to reassure them. "That's all right, gentlemen, he'll testify that he was keeping a sharp lookout. Won't you, Sam?" "No," said Sam, "I guess I can't do that."

And then, this lawyer said, such a storm of indignation burst over Sam as he had never seen. The Captain and the rest of the crew cursed him for betraying his ship. Let him go to the head if he had to. Let him even have his smoke if he must. But when he did let him also take the consequences. The collision was not his fault, they agreed. The fog may have been too thick for him to have seen the other vessel in time, but was he now going to let his own ship down? If he left his post on his own affairs, he had no right to make the ship pay the penalty. What if it was perjury? He'd taken that risk. Not the ship, but he, had taken the risk of perjury.

The admiralty lawyers sat back and listened. They recognized that there were peculiarities in the ethics of the sea which were distinctly not a part of admiralty law. The meeting broke up with Sam still obstinately refusing to do what, the Captain insisted, any good seaman ought to know he was in honor bound to do.

I tried to find a situation in which a lawyer is in duty bound to lie for his client. I asked an eminent and very practical judge. He told me he hoped I was joking. I went to two leaders of the bar, both ex-presidents of bar associations. One said, "No, I don't believe there is such a situation." The other said, "Why, of course, there are." But he has not yet given me one.

Finally I thought I had one. It was the case of a lawyer who, I felt very sure, had lied to me when he told me that he did not represent a certain man. As secretary of the Grievance Committee of the Bar Association at the time, I was trying to find out whether this man had been blackmailed by some other lawyers. I went to this lawyer and asked him. If he had admitted to me that he had represented this man, I should have been pretty sure that the man had indeed been blackmailed, for I knew that he had not gone to his regular counsel, but to a different lawyer, in order to keep the whole affair secret. The lawyer told me he did not even know the man.

I recall thinking then that this lawyer was doing just right by lying to me, but my lawyer went on to make the same denial to the Grievance Committee, and later, when the Bar Association brought proceedings for his disbarment, in the course of those proceedings, persisted in his denial before the court itself. He was not disbarred, but he was subsequently reprimanded and suspended.[14]

It was inadmissible for him not to tell the truth to the court. A lawyer's duty to his client cannot rise higher than its source, which is the court. I think he did right to lie to me, but I don't think he should have lied to the Grievance Committee as well, for it had a right to ask him. With me he was properly playing for time to see what it was all about, for I had no obvious authority.

It may be that it all depends on whether your lawyer is asked the question by someone who has a right to ask it. If he has no right to ask and if simple silence would, or even might, lead him to the truth, then, I believe your lawyer is in duty bound to lie. For the truth is not his, but yours. It belongs to you, and he is bound to keep it for you even more vigorously than if it were only his own. He must lie, then, beyond the point where he could permissibly lie for himself.

A lawyer is called on the telephone by a former client who is unfortunately at the time a fugitive from justice. The police want him, and he wants advice. The lawyer goes to where his client is, hears the whole story, and advises him to surrender. Finally he succeeds in persuading him that this is the best thing to do and they make

an appointment to go to police headquarters. Meanwhile the client
is to have two days to wind up his affairs and make his farewells.
When the lawyer gets back to his office, a police inspector is waiting
for him, and asks him whether his client is in town and where he is.

What does the lawyer do? What should he say? I have had three
interesting suggestions. The best, if it would work, was for the lawyer to say, "Don't you wish you knew!" or something like that. But
what if it didn't work, and the police inspector insisted? In that
case, says James E. Harpster, the lawyer would be "morally bound
to answer the policeman truthfully. For it seems to us that the police
have the right to know the whereabouts of wanted criminals." [15]
I wonder. Criminals have rights too, and one of them is the right
to counsel. The problem is not so easy.

The most authoritative suggestion came from the chairman of the
Committee on Professional Ethics of the American Bar Association,
Mr. Henry S. Drinker. In his learned and able, as well as authoritative, reply to my article in the *Stanford Law Review*, which was published in the next number, in April 1952, Mr. Drinker says, "When
the police officers asked the lawyer, there was no necessity for him
to lie. He should have said: 'If I knew, my duty as a lawyer would
forbid my telling you.'" [16] The clear implication is that he did not
know, and I don't see that Mr. Drinker's reply is very different
from what I think the lawyer should have said, which is simply,
"I don't know." But he did know. He had just come from where his
client was and his client had agreed to meet him two days later.

It was certainly not the lawyer's duty to disclose his client's whereabouts. Whatever others may think, lawyers will agree to that. Mr.
Drinker's Committee on Professional Ethics has been quite definite
about it. It once had the following facts presented to it: A lawyer's
client was a fugitive from justice. He jumped bail, forfeited his
bond, and a warrant was issued for his arrest. The lawyer learned
in confidence from the client's relatives where he was and advised
his client to give himself up, which eventually he did. But he refused to tell the police. The question asked was whether it was "the
duty of the attorney to disclose to the prosecuting authorities the
whereabouts of a fugitive client."

The Committee was of the opinion: "It is in the public interest
that even the worst criminal should have counsel, and counsel can-

not properly perform their duties without knowing the truth. To hold that an attorney should reveal confidential information which he has obtained, by virtue of his professional employment from members of the family of the criminal, would prevent such frank disclosure as might be necessary to a proper protection of the client's interest." [17]

Now, if there was no other way of keeping his client's secret, I believe the lawyer had better be false to the truth than false to his client. The Committee on Professional Ethics, as you see, comes perilously close to agreeing with me.*

Sometimes we forget that veracity is only a part of honorable behavior. When we isolate telling the truth and put it on its own pinnacle, we neglect the larger problem. On one occasion the British Cabinet met and decided to devalue the pound the next day. When the meeting was over, the newspaper men asked Sir Stafford Cripps, the Chancellor of the Exchequer, whether the pound was going to be devalued. He said, No. The next day, after the announcement, one of the London papers called it "the immaculate deception." Sir Frederick Pollock wrote Holmes, "I never heard of any real authority for any such proposition as that one owes full disclosure of the truth to all men at all times." Holmes replied, "You know that G. Washington cannot tell a lie business was a fiction in a popular life of him by an itinerant person." [18]

A lawyer is not faced with the question whether he may find it his duty to lie, not for a client, but to a client, as a physician must

---

* I don't think the principle of law that a client's confidential communications to his attorney are privileged solves either of the problems I have raised. As I understand it, the privilege covers only a refusal to answer. I do not understand that the privilege extends far enough to make it the duty of the lawyer to take affirmative steps, such as possibly telling a falsehood, even in circumstances when they are necessary to avoid or prevent disclosure of his client's confidences.

Unless it does, the doctrine does not cover my example of the client who is a fugitive from justice and the police who ask his lawyer where his client is. For there the lawyer could not keep his client's confidence from disclosure simply by refusing to answer.

In the case of Mr. Sleeper, it is possible that under the unusual circumstances the privilege would cover the name of his client, but the general rule is that the privilege does not protect the identity of the client. See Wigmore §2313.

sometimes lie to his patient. Dr. Lawrence J. Henderson made, so far as I know, the only sensible observations on this duty of a physician. He took the position that to speak of telling the truth, the whole truth, and nothing but the truth to a patient is absurd, because it is quite impossible. He cited cancer. If a physician tells his patient that he has cancer, it is a stimulus to which there will be a response in the patient's circulatory, respiratory, and nervous system. In other words, the physician can't tell him without affecting the very condition which the physician is not only called upon to diagnose, but to cure. "I suggest, therefore," Henderson says, "that if you recognize a duty of 'telling the truth to the patient,' you range yourself outside the class of biologists with lawyers and philosophers." [19] No, a lawyer is not a biologist, nor is a lawyer retained to minister to his client's moral health. So the lawyer must tell the truth, all of it, to his client.

A parson will lie for his parishioner, a priest for his penitent, a physician for his patient. You would lie to protect your wife or your child. There are others with whom you are intimate enough, close enough, to lie for, when you would not lie for yourself. At what point do you stop lying for them? I don't know and you are not sure.

To every one of us come occasions when we don't want to tell the truth, not all of it, certainly not all of it at once, when we want to be something less than candid, a little disingenuous. Indeed, to be candid with ourselves, there are times when we deliberately and more or less justifiably undertake to tell something less or even something different, not the whole truth. Complete candor to anyone but ourselves is a virtue that belongs to the saints, and to those who have no other responsibilities. Even when we do want to tell the truth, all of it ultimately, we see no reason why we should not take our own time, tell it as skillfully and as gracefully as we can. Most of us doubt our own ability to do this as well by and for ourselves as another could do, so we go to a lawyer. He will make a better fist of it than we can.

I don't see why we must not come out roundly and say that one of the functions of a lawyer is the disagreeable duty of choosing between being false to his client or false to the truth. On rare occasions, as I think I have shown, I believe it is his duty to prefer his client to the truth, and if need be to tell a lie. Happily they are few and far between, only when his duty gets him into a corner or puts him on the spot. Day in, day out, a lawyer can be as truthful as anyone. But not so ingenuous.

A lawyer is required to be disingenuous. He is required to say things which he does not believe in. In the higher brackets of generality, he has to be freed from his own beliefs and prejudices, for they are irrelevant unless pressed into service for the client. But his insincerity does not extend to the particular. The farther what he says descends toward the particular, the more truthful he must be, except, as I have been arguing, in respect to particulars which do not belong to him because they are his client's secrets. Barring these, when he is talking for his client, a lawyer is absolved from veracity down to a certain point of particularity.

I have said that a lawyer may not lie to the court. But it may be a lawyer's duty not to speak. Let me give you a case from the autobiography of one of the most distinguished and conscientious lawyers I or any man have ever known, Samuel Williston. In his autobiography, he tells of one of his early cases.[20] His client was sued in some financial matter. The details of the claim are not important. Mr. Williston, of course, at once got his client's letter file and went through it painstakingly, sorting, arranging, and collating it. The letters, we may well believe, told the whole story, as they usually do in such a case. Trial approached, but the plaintiff's lawyers did not ask for the file or that the letters be produced. "They did not demand their production and we did not feel bound to disclose them." At the close of the trial, "In the course of his remarks the Chief Justice stated as one reason for his decision a supposed fact which I knew to be unfounded. I had in front of me a letter that showed his error. Though I have no doubt of the propriety of my behavior in keeping silent, I was somewhat uncomfortable at the time." *

---

* Mr. Drinker says that the client's privilege was the reason "that Mr. Williston could not disclose the injurious letter from the files which the client had turned over to him for examination."

I do not understand that the files were turned over to Mr. Williston only for examination, but rather for the purpose of using them in the defense of the suit. In that case, if this particular letter was a part of any correspondence

We may share his discomfort, but there is no doubt of the propriety of his behavior. I want to quote Mr. Hocker again. He went on from what he said about a trial being an adversary business to say this:

"A trial lawyer who unnecessarily discloses the contents of his file to his adversary is as much a traitor to his client as is the general traitor to his country who discloses his plan of battle to the enemy. Play your cards from close to the vest, never volunteer damaging information which you are not obliged to disclose, obtain all of the information you can extract from the other side of the case, never yield a significant advantage. By this I do not mean to suggest that a trial lawyer should be cantankerous or disagreeable. If you know that you will be obliged to produce your client for a deposition or for a medical examination, there is no sense in requiring the opposition to obtain a court order. What you know he can get by the process, and what cannot hurt you, you might as well give him with a pleasant smile and good grace. Where there is a reasonable doubt as to whether your opponent can get dangerous information, refuse with a pleasant smile and good grace, but refuse. Ask no favors of your opponent, lest this oblige you to grant one that may pinch. If you are not a fighter by disposition you should hire a fighter to try your cases." [21]

I don't know whether Mr. Williston or Mr. Hocker want any confirmation of the rectitude of their conduct, but the Committee on Professional Ethics of the American Bar Association stands behind them, five to two. A local bar association recently put up just such a situation to the committee.[22] An attorney is in court with his client, who has been convicted, when he comes up for sentence. The clerk, or whoever it is that has the criminal records, tells the judge that this man has no record, and the judge then puts him on pro-

---

in the file which Mr. Williston was to use, as it well might have been, the client would have waived the privilege.

However, the files were not protected by the privilege. Under the doctrine as set forth by Wigmore this letter file was not a communication to the attorney. This letter was "a document of the client existing before it was communicated to the attorney," and so "not within the present privilege so as to be exempt from protection." Wigmore §2318, and 2307. A party cannot avoid discovery of a document by giving it to his attorney.

bation. As a matter of fact, he has a record, and his attorney knows it. Is it the attorney's duty to speak up?

A careful casuist might want to know the source of the attorney's knowledge. Did the defendant tell him, or how else did he learn? We may assume that his knowledge came to him in the course of his professional relations with his client. Let that pass. The crucial question seemed to a majority of the committee to be whether the defendant's attorney has any reason to understand that the judge is relying on him to corroborate or correct the clerk's statement. If so, the majority of the committee thought that the attorney should ask the judge to excuse him from answering and not to rely on his personal knowledge. It is, of course, possible that the judge would leave it at that. This would depend on the circumstances, and probably on the lawyer's demeanor and the overtones in his voice. However, the majority of the committee ruled that "If the lawyer is quite clear that the court does not rely on him as corroborating, by his silence, the statement of the clerk or of his client, the lawyer is not, in our opinion, bound to speak out." [23] If he did, we will agree, so much the less lawyer he.

You will note that Williston was the attorney for the defendant in the case. The other attorney, who was trying to make a case for the plaintiff, had the burden of proof. If he had found a damaging letter in his client's file, or if Williston's client had been bringing instead of defending the suit, what then? Quite a different situation would be presented, such is our adversary system of justice. If the ugly fact belongs to the plaintiff's case, it must go in with it; and if it is so ugly that it spoils the case, then either the plaintiff must withdraw his case or his lawyer must withdraw from it. The point is, and the reason for this difference between the claim and the defense is, simply that, unless a lawyer presents all the available relevant facts, he would be presenting a different case to the court than the one which his client brought to him. A will without its codicil is not the testament. A contract without an amendment is not the agreement. But here we come to the edge of a technical precipice. What is matter of defense? Some things are strictly the business of the defendant to bring up, if he chooses. You bring suit for divorce on the ground of adultery. You tell your lawyer that you have condoned your husband's offense by living with him after you learned of it. The court may very well deny you a divorce because you have, as the law says, condoned his adultery. I am using the word in its technical sense. You may or may not have forgiven him. Need your lawyer bring out the fact that you have forgiven your husband? Or should that be left for him to bring up?

The Twenty-second Canon of Professional Ethics states that "The conduct of the lawyer before the Court and with other lawyers should be characterized by candor and fairness." This is all very well, but Williston, when he sat there with the letter in front of him, was being faithful to his client, and uncomfortable that he could not be candid with the court. If I ask you which of two girls you love the most, you are in effect declining to answer when you say, "Both." Lawyers say that the adversary process gives the court priority over the client in matters of law and the client a priority over the court in matters of fact. The distinction is familiar enough to lawyers, and it is a useful distinction once we know what they mean by it, as I will try to make clear later. The point I want to make now is that the relations which a lawyer has with his client on one hand and his court on the other are somewhat bigamous.

Here is what Williston went on to say in his autobiography. "One of the troublesome ethical questions which a young trial lawyer is confronted with is the extent to which he is bound to disclose to the court facts which are injurious to his client's case. The answer is not doubtful. The lawyer must decide when he takes a case whether it is a suitable one for him to undertake and after this decision is made, he is not justified in turning against his client by exposing injurious evidence entrusted to him. If that evidence was unknown to him when he took the case, he may sometimes withdraw from it, but while he is engaged as counsel he is not only not obliged to disclose unfavorable evidence, but it is a violation of his duty to his client if he does so." And Williston concluded, ". . . doing something intrinsically regrettable, because the only alternative involves worse consequences, is a necessity in every profession." [24]

It was a question, he said, of moral compromise, and he referred to a passage in Lecky's *The Map of Life*. This passage is worth quoting:

"But at best there must be many things in the profession from which a very sensitive conscience would recoil, and things must be said and done which can hardly be justified except on the ground that the existence of this profession and the prescribed methods of its action are in the long run indispensable to the honest administration of justice." [25]

"I must be cruel, only to be kind," said Hamlet, on his way to his mother. And so likewise a lawyer has to tell himself strange things on his way to court. But they are strange only to those who do not distinguish between truth and justice. Justice is something larger and more intimate than truth. Truth is only one of the ingredients of justice. Its whole is the satisfaction of those concerned. It is to that end that each attorney must say the best, and only the best, of his own case.

This is not the method we have used in other endeavors, with not only more, but with conspicuous success. But the law has other things than success to think about. It must give the losing party, and his friends and his sympathizers, as much satisfaction as any loser can expect. At least the most has been said for him. The whole has been shaken out into the sun, and everyone concerned is given a feeling akin to the feeling of security which you get when you have told yourself the worst before you make a decision. The administration of justice is no more designed to elicit the truth than the scientific approach is designed to extract justice from the atom.

Advocacy requires a lawyer to start with something to be proved, and this is as true of facts as it is of propositions of law. When he goes to interview a witness as well as when he goes to the law library, he goes to get something. He will waste a lot of time if he goes with an open mind. He must, of course, first formulate the issue in his mind, but he does this only to make it the easier to find what lies on his side of the issue. He fixes on the conclusion which will best serve his client's interests, and then he sets out to persuade others to agree.

Judges do the same thing, but not on purpose. They find themselves reaching a decision before they know just how they got there. Raeburn Green has spoken of this phenomenon. He says,

"We are told by authorities of diverse experience—Mr. Justice Cardozo, Mr. Radin and Signor Calamandrei—that the course of judicial reasoning is frequently backward, from conclusion to premise. It is a course which (as has been pointed out) is familiar to the practicing lawyer, whose client often presents him with a conclusion ready-made, and who must then search for whatever premises can be discovered or developed, to support that conclusion. It is no doubt true also that the judicial practice of taking a vote following the oral argument, leaving the opinion to be written later, is frequently conducive to the inverted process.

"When the whole structure is complete in the opinion, it is naturally difficult to detect whether the roof was first erected or the supporting pillars. One would think that Mr. Justice Brandeis must have almost invariably proceeded in the orthodox fashion, from premise to conclusion, and that Mr. Justice Holmes must in some cases have proceeded in this fashion and in others in the reverse; but the fact may have been quite otherwise. For not only is the opinion deceptive, but there can also be dispute as to what is a conclusion and what is a premise. One man's premise may be another's conclusion; and every premise which is not an absolute is itself the conclusion of some syllogism, however long forgotten." [26]

Now it is quite true that our thinking is done on an alternating current, so to speak, from induction to deduction and reverse. A process which we do not clearly understand—at least no philosopher has yet explained it—induces a tentative conclusion from which we proceed deductively. This is an intellectual process. We can watch deduction work, which we cannot do with the inductive phase, and so we call it intuitive, by which we mean only that we cannot watch it work. It is none the less a fact, as Cardozo, whom Green cites, and others in other lines of work have recognized.

In *Paradoxes of Legal Science,* Cardozo writes,

"For the creative process in law, and indeed in science generally, has a kinship to the creative process in art. Imagination, whether you call it scientific or artistic, is for each the faculty that creates. There are successive stages of preparation, incubation and illumination described with so much insight by Graham Wallas in his analysis of the art of thought. Learning is indeed necessary, but learning (to paraphrase what has been said of Keats) is the springboard by which imagination leaps to truth. The law has its piercing intuitions, its tense, apocalyptic moments. We gather together our principles and precedents and analogies, even at times our fictions, and summon them to yield the energy that will best attain the jural end. If our wand has the divining touch, it will seldom knock in vain. So it is that the conclusion, however deliberate and labored, has often the aspect in the end of nothing but a lucky find. 'When I once asked the best administrator whom I knew,' writes Mr. Wallas, 'how he formed his decisions, he laughed, and with the air of letting out for the first time a guilty secret, said: "Oh, I always decide by feeling. So and so always decides by calculation, and that is no good." When, again, I asked an American judge, who is widely admired both for his skill and for his impartiality, how he and his fellows formed their conclusions, he also laughed, and said that he should be stoned in the street if it were known that, after listening with full consciousness to all the evidence, and following as carefully as he could all the arguments, he waited until he "felt" one way or the other.' He had elided the preparation and the brooding, or at least had come to think of them as processes of faint kinship with the state of mind that followed. 'When the conclusion is there,' said William James, 'we have always forgotten most of the steps preceding its attainment.' " [27]

The same thing is true of physicians. Lawrence J. Henderson said, "More often than not, skillful diagnosticians reach a diagnosis before they are aware, or at any rate, conscious, of the grounds that justify their decision. If asked to explain the reasons for the diagnosis, they often clearly show by their behavior that they are obliged to think them out, and that to do so is an awkward task. This is true of doctors, of lawyers, and of men of affairs." [28] And it is equally true of the investment analyst and advisor, according to one of the best of them. In *Security Analysis,* Graham has an appendix in which he compares his work with the work of a physician in the light of Henderson's remarks, finding an analogy between the patient and the security.[29] I think we may take what Henderson says as common to all pursuits in which the discipline is not capable of being strict and the pursuit not completely successful.

This is an unconscionably long assertion of the inexplicable. So far as the lawyer is concerned, a single remark from a scientist should content you. Charles Darwin said, "How odd it is that anyone should not see that all observation must be for or against some view if it is to be of any service!" [30] You have to be as eager in your thinking as in anything else. In other words, you have to be an advocate. Of course, I recognize that this demands a counter-weight of candor to yourself. But neither eagerness nor advocacy makes candor to yourself impossible. And equilibrium is easier as well as more stable between two distant and opposed forces than when anything, big or little, is precariously balanced on the center of the seesaw.

I was once chairman of a commission to recommend revisions in the workmen's compensation law of Massachusetts. We opened our deliberations with a meeting which was open to the public. A man spoke up from the back of the hall and said he was glad that the chairman was impartial. He was referring to the fact that the other members of the commission were drawn from labor and management. I brightened at the compliment, however obvious, and thanked him. I assured him that I was indeed impartial, at any rate for the time being. I had, I said, the pure impartiality of complete ignorance, and I hoped that it would not last. I hoped that it would be gone before we had to make our report.

There are those who admire what they call objectivity, and journalists, in their asceticism, as well as lawyers are properly interested. The Nieman Fellows at Harvard held a symposium a few years ago on the question of whether a newspaperman could interpret the news and still retain his objectivity. One of the symposiasts pointed out that objectivity could be "carried to the point of unintelligibility." He gave an example—I forget what it was—of what he called "strictly factual" writing, and said, "And so it is. There is no slant, no bias, no prejudice. You just can't understand it." [31]

Karl Llewellyn has shrewdly pointed out the consequence of having the conclusion given to you and predetermined. It requires lawyers to rely solely upon the power of persuasion. No authority. Only persuasion. He says, "Now the advocate is the one peculiar thinker about problems whose *conclusion is always given*. On this, his only choice is whether he will refuse to take the case, either because he does not like the case or because he cannot find premises to support it. *If* he takes it, even to work on, he starts his thinking *by trade necessity* with his conclusion. What direct relevance has judicial or counsellor's predictive thinking to such a peculiar thought-process? Other thinkers seek for the conclusion. But the emphasis, for advocates' thinking, is and must be always: *given* my conclusion, how can I develop a *persuasive* line of premise, and how can I *persuade* my premises into *acceptance by the tribunal?*" [32]

Lawyers have great respect for authority perhaps just because they exercise none. They argue to the court and to the jury. They advise their clients, and their clients need not take their advice. There are other lawyers. Indeed there are other advisers. A good lawyer is so persuasive that we forget that he has no more authority over a client than he has over the court. A successful businessman, an executive, on the other hand, gets so used to authority, even over his board of directors, that he forgets the skills of persuasion. This is the businessman's great handicap in politics. A congressional committee has little, very little, in common with a board of directors, or even a majority stockholder. It is only the executive who has been brought up through the sales department who retains even the rudiments of the art of persuasion.

You will not think me irreverent, nor, I hope, presumptuous, if I offer you Plato's Supreme Craftsman as analogous. He was not omnipotent. He was not coercive. He was persuasive. Plato's "final conviction," Whitehead says, "towards the end of his life," was "that the divine element in the world is to be conceived as a persuasive agency and not as a coercive agency. This doctrine should be looked upon as one of the greatest intellectual discoveries in the history of religion. . . The alternative doctrine, prevalent then and now, sees either in the many gods or in the one God, the final coercive forces wielding the thunder." [33]

The Guilty Client

The problem presented to a lawyer when he defends a man he knows is guilty or takes a case he knows is bad is perplexing only to laymen. Brandeis said, "As a practical matter, I think the lawyer is not often harassed by this problem, partly because he is apt to believe at the time in most of the cases that he actually tries, and partly because he either abandons or settles a large number of those he does not believe in." [34]

It is profoundly true that the first person a lawyer persuades is himself. A practicing lawyer will soon detect in himself a perfectly astonishing amount of sincerity. By the time he has even sketched out his brief, however skeptically he started, he finds himself believing more and more in what it says, until later, when he starts arguing the case before the court, his belief is total; and he is quite sincere about it. You cannot very well keep your tongue in your cheek while you are talking. He believes what he is saying in a way that will later astonish himself as much as now it does others.[35]

Not that he cares how much we are astonished. What he does care about is whether we are persuaded, and he is aware that an unsound argument can do much worse than fall flat. For it may carry the implication that he has no better one. He will not want to make it unless he really has no better.

This sort of self-sown sincerity, however, is not deep-rooted; and it had better not be, if what Justice Darling said was true. "I think," he said, "that most Counsel would be better advocates did they content themselves with simulating the belief instead of actually embracing it. The manifest appearance of a believer is all that is wanted; and this can well be acted after a little study, and will not interfere with that calmness of judgment which it is well to preserve in the midst of uncertainties, and which does not appear to be consistent with much faith." [36] "Better advocates," Justice Darling says, not better men. I trust you understand that I am drawing a distinction which I have no doubt Justice Darling would draw too, and equally emphatically. I am talking about cases, not about causes. I am not talking about the integrity and righteousness on which our best hopes hang. This is vicarious zeal and enthusiasm, not one's own belief. To be truly honest, you've got to be honest, not only with yourself, but also for yourself. At some time or other, you stand alone. We are bipeds, which means we must stand on our own two feet, not on the four feet we may make with another.

This is more than a domestic problem. It strikes close to the best the bar can do for the community, as the bar very well knows. The trouble is, there is also the right of a lawyer to take only the cases he wants to take. It is the same problem of reconciling two confronting rights which festers in racial discrimination. There is the right to choose whom you prefer to employ confronting the right to a job on something better than the color of your skin. Likewise a lawyer's right to choose his clients confronts a free man's right to counsel. The bar, as I say, is wholly aware of this. Just this year, the foremost bar association we have, the Association of the Bar of the City of New York, made this matter clear. Its Committee on the Bill of Rights, whose chairman is George S. Leisure, said this, "A principal duty of the bar is to see that no accused lacks counsel because his person is infamous or his cause detested. When a member of the bar defends a client who is publicly abhorred, the bar expects that representation none the less to be vigorous, competent and responsible in every way. The bar regards that lawyer as fundamentally independent of his client and therefore holds him accountable to it for guiding his client's cause by its standards of professional conduct. Public misapprehension of the duty threatens its performance. The prevalence of the error, too often reflected in our local press, which confuses professional obligation with personal belief, will deter lawyers from representing unpopular clients. The organized bar should act to dispel such misunderstanding, and should support against criticism arising from it those lawyers who, guided by the profession's standards, follow its most honored tradition and help discharge its most essential responsibility." [37]

The classical solution to a lawyer taking a case he knows is bad is Dr. Johnson's. It is perfectly simple and quite specious. Boswell asked Johnson whether as a moralist Johnson did not think that the practice of the law, in some degree, hurt the nice feeling of honesty. "What do you think," said Boswell, "of supporting a cause which you know to be bad?"

Johnson answered, "Sir, you do not know it to be good or bad till the Judge determines it. I have said that you are to state facts fairly; so that your thinking, or what you call knowing, a cause to be bad, must be from reasoning, must be from your supposing your arguments to be weak and inconclusive. But, Sir, that is not enough. An argument which does not convince yourself, may convince the Judge to whom you urge it: and if it does convince him, why, then, Sir, you are wrong, and he is right." [38]

Dr. Johnson ignored the fact that it is the lawyer's job to know how good or how bad his case is. It is his peculiar function to find out, for otherwise he can't make it look better. Dr. Johnson's answer is sound only in cases where the problem does not arise. It is not the lawyer, but the law, that does not know whether his case is good or bad. The law is trying to find out, and so wants everyone defended and every debatable case tried. To this end, the law tries

to make it easy for a lawyer to take a bad case, whether it's bad in
the relevant sense of looking hopeless, or bad in the irrelevant sense
of being unpopular, perhaps even deliberately made offensive by the
capering of some Congressional Committee.

In England, the law goes so far as to make it the duty of a bar-
rister to take the case of any client who properly and adequately
retains him. In this country we lay that duty upon the bar as a
whole, and so we don't try to do more than make it as easy as we
can for a lawyer to take a bad case. One of the ways the bar helps
itself to perform this duty is the Canon of Ethics which says, "It is
improper for a lawyer to assert in argument his personal belief in
his client's innocence or in the justice of his cause." [39] It is called
improper just so that the lawyer may feel that he does not have to.
This, I think, must be its only purpose, for it is honored in no other
way, as you will agree if you have ever heard a lawyer argue a case
which he has chosen to turn into a cause. How else would you have
your lawyer argue any case to a jury or a constitutional case to the
Supreme Court?

Listen to George Wharton Pepper's peroration to his argument
to the Supreme Court on a constitutional question.[40] Having argued
in the most precise terms that the AAA is unconstitutional, he proceeds most eloquently to express his own personal belief in the justice of his cause. "My time is fleeting and I must not pause to sum
up the argument I have made. . . But I do want to say just one final
and somewhat personal word. I have tried very hard to argue this
case calmly and dispassionately, and without vehement attack upon
things which I cannot approve, and I have done it thus because it
seems to me that this is the best way in which an advocate can discharge his duty to this Court. But I do not want your Honors to
think that my feelings are not involved, and that my emotions are
not deeply stirred. Indeed, may it please Your Honors, I believe I
am standing here today to plead the cause of the America I have
loved; and I pray Almighty God that not in my time may 'the
land of the regimented' be accepted as a worthy substitute for 'the
land of the free.' " [41]

To be sure, constitutional law is less law than it is politics and
statesmanship. As if the best of the one was not as good as the
other! But here is a canon which calls improper something which

the most proper lawyers do. I suggest that its only purpose is to relieve lawyers of the necessity of expressing their opinion, so that they may never need express it unless they want to express it, and keep it to themselves whenever they choose. The canon gives a lawyer an excuse when his client wants him to espouse a cause, when all the lawyer wants to take is a case.

No, there is nothing unethical in taking a bad case or defending the guilty or advocating what you don't believe in. It is ethically neutral. It's a free choice. There is a Daumier drawing of a lawyer arguing, a very demure young woman sitting near him, and a small boy beside her sucking a lollypop. The caption says, "He defends the widow and the orphan, unless he is attacking the orphan and the widow." It is hanging in my office. It was given to me by a lady whose case I did not want to take.

I am not being cynical. We are not dealing with the morals which govern a man acting for himself, but with the ethics of advocacy. We are talking about the special moral code which governs a man who is acting for another. Lawyers in their practice—how they behave elsewhere does not concern us—put off more and more of our common morals the farther they go in a profession which treats right and wrong, vice and virtue, on such equal terms. Some lawyers find nothing to take its place. There are others who put on new and shining raiment.

I will give you as good an example as I know that a lawyer can make a case as noble as a cause. I want to tell you how Arthur D. Hill came into the Sacco-Vanzetti case. It was through Felix Frankfurter, and it is his story. Frankfurter wrote some of it in the newspapers shortly after Arthur's death, and he told it to me in more detail just after the funeral.

When the conviction of Sacco and Vanzetti had been sustained by the Supreme Judicial Court of Massachusetts, there was left an all but hopeless appeal to the federal courts, that is, to the Supreme Court. "It was at this stage," Felix Frankfurter said, "that I was asked if I would try to enlist Arthur Hill's legal services to undertake a final effort on behalf of the men, hopeless as it seemed, by appeal to the Federal law."

Frankfurter called Arthur Hill up and said that he had a very serious matter to discuss with him. "In that case," said Arthur Hill, "we had better have a good lunch first. I will meet you at the Somerset Club for lunch and afterwards you will tell me about it." They lunched together at the Somerset Club, then after lunch crossed Beacon Street and sat on a bench in Boston Common overlooking the Frog Pond. And Frankfurter asked Arthur Hill if he would undertake this final appeal of the Sacco-Vanzetti case to the Supreme Court.

Arthur Hill said, "If the president of the biggest bank in Boston came to me and said that his wife had been convicted of murder, but he wanted me to see if there was any possible relief in the Supreme Court of the United States and offered me a fee of $50,000 to make such an effort, of course I would take the retainer as would, I suppose, everybody else at the bar. It would be a perfectly honorable thing to see whether there was anything in the record which laid a basis for an appeal to the Federal Court.

"I do not see how I can decline a similar effort on behalf of Sacco and Vanzetti simply because they are poor devils against whom the feeling of the community is strong and they have no money with which to hire me. I don't particularly enjoy the proceedings that will follow, but I don't see how I can possibly refuse to make the effort."

Arthur Hill took it as a law case. To him it was a case, not a cause. He was not the partisan, he was the advocate. I want to add just one other thing, which Arthur Hill said to me, years later. It sets a sort of seal upon his conduct in the case, as a case, and not a cause. I used to meet him fairly often walking downtown, because we both often stopped at the Boston Athenaeum and we would go on downtown together. One morning I was stupid enough to ask him an indiscreet question. I had expressed my own opinion on the guilt or innocence of Sacco and Vanzetti. I said I thought that on the whole it seemed to me probable that they had been guilty, and asked Arthur what he thought. Arthur looked at me—it was years later, twenty years later—smiled, and said, "I have never said, and I cannot say, what I think on that subject because, you see, Charlie, I was their counsel."

I met Judge Thayer once. This, too, was some years after the trial. We were in his chambers in Boston settling an automobile accident case then on trial before him. We were all standing, and he was standing between me and the window, so that when I looked out the window behind him I saw the top of the Charlestown Jail where the death house was in the background of a sort of living portrait of Judge Thayer framed by the window. I wasn't thinking anything much about it until I realized that Judge Thayer was no longer talking about our case, but strutting up and down and boasting that he had been fortunate enough to be on the bench when those sons of bitches were convicted. I had a chill, and I comforted and warmed myself over thoughts of Arthur Hill.

I have talked lovingly about the practice of the law. I have spoken unsparingly, as I would to another lawyer. In a way the practice of the law is like free speech. It defends what we hate as well as what we most love. For every lawyer whose conscience may be pricked, there is another whose virtue is tickled. Every case has two sides, and for every lawyer on the wrong side, there's another on the right side. I don't know any other career that offers an ampler opportunity for both the enjoyment of virtue and the exercise of vice, or, if you please, the exercise of virtue and the enjoyment of vice, except possibly the ancient rituals which were performed in some temples by vestal virgins, in others by sacred prostitutes.

Devotion and Detachment

Let us now go back and reconsider, perhaps reconstruct, this entire devotion which a lawyer owes to his client.

The fact is, the devotion is not entire. The full discharge of a lawyer's duty to his client requires him to withhold something. If a lawyer is entirely devoted to his client, his client receives something less than he has a right to expect. For, if a man devotes the whole of himself to another, he mutilates or diminishes himself, and the other receives the devotion of so much the less. This is no paradox, but a simple calculus of the spirit.

Good lawyers know this. It was true of Brandeis. His appointment to the Supreme Court was opposed for his sharp practices at the bar, for being a ruthless and unscrupulous advocate, for taking cases against former clients. So his opponents said. And yet Austen G. Fox, who led the fight against his confirmation by the Senate before the Senate subcommittee is quoted as saying, "The trouble with Mr. Brandeis is that he never loses his judicial attitude toward his clients. He always acts the part of a judge toward his clients instead of being his client's lawyer, which is against the practices of the Bar." [42] This remark loses nothing in Fox's obvious disapproval. Frederick P. Fish would never own any stock in a client's corporation. He said that he "never invested in a client." He would no more do that than a judge would hold stock in a corporation which was a party in a case before him.

Let me cite a third lawyer, for his name is synonymous with one of the great New York law firms. Robert T. Swaine, in his history of the Cravath firm, wrote that Paul D. Cravath "early came to believe that in most cases the client is best advised by a lawyer who maintains an objective point of view and that such objectivity may be impeded by any financial interest in the client's business or any participation in its management. Accordingly, he made it the policy of the firm that neither its partners nor its associates should hold equity securities of any client, or serve as a director of a corporate client, or have a financial interest, direct or indirect, in any transaction in which the firm was acting as counsel. Occasionally, more frequently in recent years, clients have insisted upon exceptions permitting partners to occupy directorships and own qualifying equity securities, but the exceptions have been few." [43]

It takes nothing from the wisdom of Cravath's policy that it was based on experience. Swaine adds, "It was Cravath's experience in the Metropolitan matter that led to the rule that no member of the firm or staff may be a director of a corporate client, save in exceptional cases." [44] This was an unfortunate experience. Cravath was sued as a director in the Metropolitan Securities matter for an allegedly illegal redemption of some debentures. The suit was settled. Swaine gives a detailed account of the whole affair.[45]

Fish and Brandeis and Cravath knew that they could not give their clients the full measure of their devotion unless they kept themselves detached. Thereby they were able to offer their clients what they had come to get—advice and counsel from someone above the turmoil of their troubles or at least far enough away from them to look at them. By not putting their emotions as well as their minds up for hire, they saved, for the clients as well as for themselves, the waste of spirit which some lawyers confuse with devotion.

There is authority for such detachment. It is not Christian. Nor is the practice of law a characteristically Christian pursuit. The practice of law is vicarious, not altruistic, and the lawyer must go back of Christianity to Stoicism for the vicarious detachment which will permit him to serve his client.

E. R. Bevan, in his *Stoics and Sceptics*, summarized the Stoic faith as follows: "The Wise Man was not to concern himself with his brethren . . . he was only to serve them. Benevolence he was to have, as much of it as you can conceive; but there was one thing he must not have, and that was love. . . He must do everything which it is possible for him to do, shrink from no extreme of physical pain, in order to help, to comfort, to guide his fellow men, but whether he succeeds or not must be a matter of pure indifference to him. If he has done his best to help you and failed, he will be perfectly satisfied with having done his best. The fact that you are no better off for his exertions will not matter to him at all. Pity, in the sense of a painful emotion caused by the sight of other men's suffering, is actually a vice. . . In the service of his fellow men he must be prepared to sacrifice his life; but there is one thing he must never sacrifice: his own eternal calm." [46]

But let the greatest modern Stoic of them all, because he outgrew it, tell us about himself. "I have been able," Montaigne said, "to concern myself with public affairs without moving the length of my nail from myself, and give myself to others without taking anything from myself. . . We carry ill what possesses and carries us. Anyone who uses only his own judgment and address proceeds more gaily. He feints, he ducks, he counters at his ease, and according to the needs of the occasion. When he misses, it is without torment, without affliction, ready and whole for a new enterprise. The bridle is in his hand." And further on, "The mayor and Montaigne have always been two people, clearly separated. There's no reason why a lawyer or a banker should not recognize the knavery that is part of his vocation. An honest man is not responsible for the vices or the stupidity of his calling, and need not refuse to practise them. They are customs in his country and there is profit in them. A man must live in the world and avail himself of what he finds there." [47]

The Stoics gave us a counsel of frigid perfection, but it is none the less valid. If a lawyer is to be the best lawyer he is capable of being and discharge his entire duty to his clients, here in the Stoic sage is his exemplar. Here in Stoicism is his philosophy. Let him be a Christian, if he choose, outside the practice of the law, but in his relations with his clients, let him be a Stoic, for the better Stoic, the better lawyer.

It is at this point that I get confused between vicarious conduct and altruistic conduct. Vicarious conduct strikes me as characteristically Stoic, as altruistic conduct is characteristically Christian. However that may be, let me try to explain my confusion away. When you act vicariously, you act instead of another. You act in his behalf. It is necessarily a three-way, a triadic, relation, for there are outsiders with whom you are dealing for the other, as a lawyer deals with others for his client. On the other hand, altruistic conduct is only two-way, essentially dyadic. It ignores the outsiders. There are only two people in the picture. You act for the other, but only for his benefit. You are doing unto him what you would like him to do unto you, and so make the relation symmetrical. My confusion, I think, arose from the fact that both modes of action are contraries of the egotistical, and from the further fact that there is an altruistic element in any vicarious act. They must be distinguished, but they cannot be separated. The lawyer is acting for the good of his client as well as in his behalf. So there is a Christian element in his lawyer's Stoicism, but I maintain that the true lawyerlike lawyer is predominantly a Stoic. There remains the vastly more important question of the relation of both modes of action to coöperation, which I don't undertake to explain because I don't understand it. What we are concerned with now is the relation between the vicarious and the egotistical, between acting in behalf of another and being only yourself. This requires us to distinguish and try to set aside the corresponding relation between altruism and egotism. All I know about that relation is what Emerson said in his journal, "Take egotism out, and you would castrate the benefactors." [48]

A lawyer should treat his cases like a vivid novel, and identify himself with his client no more than he does with the hero or the heroine in the plot. Then he will work with "the zest that most people feel under their concern when they assist at existing emergencies, not actually their own; or join in facing crises that are grave, but for somebody else." I can't put it more neatly than Cozzens.[49] I can only add that this zest may deepen into a peculiar and almost spiritual satisfaction, as wide as it is deep. He will be taking T. S. Eliot's advice to readers of Dante. "You are not called upon to believe what Dante believed, for your belief will not give you a groat's worth more of understanding and appreciation; but you are called upon more and more to understand it. If you can read poetry as poetry, you will 'believe' in Dante's theology exactly as you believe in the physical reality of his journey; that is, you suspend both belief and disbelief. . . What is necessary to appreciate the poetry of the *Purgatorio* is not belief, but suspension of belief." [50]

How is a lawyer to secure this detachment? There are two ways of doing it, two devices, and all lawyers, almost all, are familiar with one or the other of them.

One way is to treat the whole thing as a game. I am not talking about the sporting theory of justice, in which it is the judge who treats his job as if it were a game. That is a caricature of the adversary system. I am talking about a lawyer's personal relations with his client. I am thinking about the necessity of his detaching himself from his client. Never blame a lawyer for treating litigation as a game, however much you may blame the judge. The lawyer is detaching himself. A man who has devoted his life to taking on other people's troubles would be swamped by them if he were to adopt them as his own. He must stay on the upland of his own personality, not only to protect himself, but in order to give his client the very thing that his client came for, as Brandeis and Fish and Cravath and Montaigne so well understood.

I must refer again to the Stoics. In Gilbert Murray's small lively book, *The Stoic Philosophy*, he says, "Life becomes, as the Stoics more than once tell us, like a play which is acted or a game played with counters. Viewed from outside, the counters are valueless; but to those engaged in the game their importance is paramount. What really and ultimately matters is that the game shall be played as it should be played. God, the eternal dramatist, has cast you for some part in His drama, and hands you the *rôle*. It may turn out that you are cast for a triumphant king; it may be for a slave who dies of torture. What does that matter to the good actor? He can play either part; his only business is to accept the *rôle* given him, and to perform it well. Similarly, life is a game of counters. Your business is to play it in the right way. He who set the board may have given

you many counters; he may have given you few. He may have ar-
ranged that, at a particular point in the game, most of your men
shall be swept accidentally off the board. You will lose the game;
but why should you mind that? It is your play that matters, not
the score that you happen to make. He is not a fool to judge you
by your mere success or failure. Success or failure is a thing He
can determine without stirring a hand. It hardly interests Him.
What interests Him is the one thing which He cannot determine—
the action of your free and conscious will." [51]

But this is not a Stoic monopoly. "I want you to understand,"
Yeats wrote, "that once one makes a thing subject to reason, as
distinguished from impulse, one plays with it, even if it is a very
serious thing. I am more ashamed because of the things I have
played with in life than of any other things." [52] Yeats was no Stoic,
as his shame shows.

The other way is a sense of craftsmanship. Perhaps it comes to the
same thing, but I think not quite. There is a satisfaction in playing
a game the best you can, as there is in doing anything else as well
as you can, which is quite distinct from making a good score.

> "Who can put life into . . . ? Let us not brawl—
> But—No joy in crafts-goal well won?
> No pleasure in pitching a neatly curved ball?
> No fun in the fact that good doing is fun,
> That races, in part, are just there to be run? [53]

A lawyer may have to treat the practice of law as if it were a game,
but if he can rely on craftsmanship, it may become an art, and "Art,
being bartender, is never drunk; And Magic that believes itself,
must die." [54] "Who sweeps a room, as for thy laws, Makes that and
the action fine." [55] I wonder if there is anything more exalted than
the intense pleasure of doing a job as well as you can irrespective
of its usefulness or even of its purpose. At least it's a comfort.

The Art of Relevance

What is this craft, the lawyer's craft? "If lawyers are true to
their function," Frankfurter told the American Law Institute, and
he has often recurred to this point, "then they are what I venture

to call experts in relevance. And an expert in relevance is a person who has intellectual disinterestedness, who penetrates a problem as far as the human mind dealing with affairs is capable of penetrating, and who is free, who is not entangled in exercising a fair judgment and is not thwarted by personal, partial or parochial interests." [56]

You must strike at the jugular, as Holmes was fond of saying, and his metaphor lies behind Frankfurter's art of the relevant. The point is, a lawyer knows better how to ask the right question than anyone who thinks he already knows the answer. We have learned the answers, all the answers. It is the questions that we do not know. "We are not wise." [57]

And a lawyer, a good lawyer, needs to be wise. For he can't possibly know enough to meet the occasions which are constantly confronting him. I know a very distinguished lawyer who told me how once he went to call on an old lawyer friend of his who was sick. This friend was an older man who had been a leader of the bar and almost as distinguished. He looked up, pleased at my friend's visit, and asked, "Do you know what I've been thinking while I've been lying here? I've been trying to think of any occasion in a man's life when he would not be better off for a lawyer's advice. I can't think of any."

"Other men are specialists," Dr. Watson said. "Holmes' specialty is omniscience." There is only one substitute for omniscience, short of the miraculous. It is the art of the relevant. I want you to hear a man of science describe the scientific method and ask you if it is not precisely the same thing.

Percy W. Bridgman, a Nobel prize winner who is as thoughtful as he is successful, says, "I like to say that there is no scientific method as such, but that the most vital feature of the scientist's procedure has been merely to do his utmost with his mind, *no holds barred*. This means in particular that no special privileges are accorded to authority or to tradition, that personal prejudices and predilections are carefully guarded against, that one makes continued check to assure oneself that one is not making mistakes, and that any line of inquiry will be followed that appears at all promising." [58]

Tell me if you see any difference between what the scientist says about his work and what Frankfurter, the judge, says about his.

Of course I can't define such a craft as this, but I know some of the things it includes. It is not only asking the right question. There is the prior question, too seldom asked, whether you are not really asking, not for the answer, but for who should give the answer, or indeed who must give it, for so often no one else ought to be asked. Again a lawyer knows that a proposition or a proposal may often be better tested by contrasting its contrary than by comparing whatever plausible and attractive variation seems to be the alternative. For a lawyer can distinguish between contraries and subcontraries, that is, between the either/or and its cousin, the more of this versus the less of that. And this too, though perhaps it is the same thing, between questions where the consequences of a different answer are the less different or the more different the harder it is to decide which answer to give. They know, perhaps they learned it from their Stoic predecessors, what is within their power and what is not. They know how soon they must be content to stop short of the best answer by an urgency of decision which requires them to accept the second best. They know that neither truth nor wisdom necessarily lie between the two extremes which to them seem falsehood or folly. They know that the more certain something seems, the more warily it must be approached and the more tenderly handled.

I am dabbing at a subject too large to trifle with, and I don't know enough to do more. All I really know is that there must be some talent which the expert in a special field lacks when he talks nonsense outside of it and which enables the man who is not a specialist, and knows he's not, to make sense about what he knows little about. But I confess that what the old lawyer said is plucking at my ear, and perhaps this is why I want to go on.

I think that this craft of the relevant, this diagnostic skill, comes only of experience that amounts to familiarity. Henderson went on, after speaking of the diagnosticians who reach a diagnosis before they are conscious of the grounds which justify it, to call this "one mark of a kind of skill, hardly ever learned except by long practice, that is indispensable in the interpretation of what men say.

"The probability that a diagnosis is correct, is less than the probability that a careful deduction from accurate measurements is correct. But when better ways do not avail, experience shows that the conclusions of the skilled diagnostician may be cautiously used with good results even for scientific purposes. Not less important is the fact that practice in diagnosis is a means of becoming thoroughly familiar with the material in which one works and that skill in diagnosis is an unmistakable sign of that familiarity." [59] Elsewhere Henderson added, "The physician must have, first, intimate, habitual, intuitive familiarity with things; secondly, systematic knowledge of things; and thirdly, an effective way of thinking about things. His intuitive familiarity must embrace his systematic knowledge and his way of thinking as well as the things he studies." [60] It is a technique that has become intuitive, not an intuition which we have turned into an intellectual process. It is a knack that is born of experience.[61]

Ruskin said of Turner, the painter, that he did right only when he ceased to reflect, was powerful only when he made no effort, and successful only when he had taken no aim.[62] And Emerson, that the Greeks "cut the Pentilican marble as if it were snow, and their perfect works in architecture and sculpture seemed things of course, not more difficult than the completion of a new ship at the Medford yards, or new mills at Lowell. These things are in course, may be taken for granted." [63]

Do you think that you do your best when you exert your best effort? It is not so. Your best is done as a matter of course, when you scarcely know that you are exerting yourself, when you are least conscious of the effort. For example, when you act in anger. There are occasions, as Blake said, when "the tigers of wrath are wiser than the horses of instruction." It is not that you do not make an effort, but most of the effort is long past. You have been making it for a long time now. Almost, what you are doing now as a matter of course, you find it impossible not to do. Almost you cannot help doing it. This, I think, is the explanation of Holmes's paradox that only by our best efforts do we attain the inevitable. Our efforts pile up so high a head behind what we are doing that it becomes inevitable that we should do it.

Why? What is the reason? Is it for the same reason that some things cannot be taught, at least not explicitly in lessons? No one learns ethics by being taught them as something outside of himself, as law. They can become part of him only by example and by shared experience. Again, is the great power of the implicit major premise, the implied assumption, the same thing? As soon as we make it explicit, it seems somehow to lose its force. I think they are parallel phenomena, but I do not know how far apart they are.

It is hard not to ask the reason. I suggest that what I am trying to say is the coöperation of the whole of you, and that the efficacy of what I have called the matter of course, resides in the fact that the whole of you is bent to the task. You are unaware of the effort you are making, because none of you is left to watch you. Or perhaps because a man can watch himself only part by part, serially. When a man is fully conscious of what he is doing, there is too little of him left to do it. You can put the whole of yourself to work only when part of you is not watching you. "Mein kind, ich hab' es klug gemacht: Ich habe nie uber das Denken gedacht." Or, if I may translate Goethe, "My boy, I'll say that I've been clever: I think, but think of thinking never." [64]

A lawyer serves his client best at heart's full length, no closer to the fire of his client's wrongs than he dares, for fear of getting scorched. How hard this is to do! And yet how necessary! Listen, if you will, to Whitehead.

"There are two contrasted ideas which seem inevitably to underlie all width of experience, one of them is the notion of importance, the sense of importance, the presupposition of importance. The other is the notion of matter-of-fact. There is no escape from sheer matter-of-fact. It is the basis of importance, and importance is important because of the inescapable character of matter-of-fact. We concentrate by reason of a sense of importance. And when we concentrate, we attend to matter-of-fact. Those people who in a hard-headed way confine their attention to matter-of-fact do so by reason of their sense of the importance of such an attitude. The two notions are antithetical, and require each other."

"A sound technological procedure is to analyze the facts in disregard of any subjective judgment as to their relative interest. And yet the notion of importance is like nature itself: Expel it with a pitch-fork, and it ever returns. The most ardent upholders of objectivity in scientific thought insist upon its importance. In truth 'to uphold a doctrine' is itself such an insistence. Apart from a feeling of interest, you would merely notice the doctrine and not uphold it. The zeal for truth presupposes interest. Also sustained observation presupposes the notion. For concentrated attention means disregard of irrelevancies, and such disregard can only be sustained by some sense of importance." [65]

I have compared the lawyer to the banker who handles other people's money and to the parson and the priest who handle other people's spiritual aspirations. Let me go farther. Compare the lawyer with the poet whose speech goes to the heart of things. "Yet he is that one especially who speaks civilly to Nature as a second person and in some sense is the patron of the world. Though more than any he stands in the midst of Nature, yet more than any he can stand aloof from her." [66]

The Lawyer

Lawyers as Legislators

You see the tractors laboring majestically across the field, cultivating the land. You don't see the earthworms. They are even less conscious of the magnitude of their achievement than the lawyers are of their part in legislation. The Congress in Washington and the legislatures in the state capitals pass laws. The administrative agencies turn out regulations. The courts hand down judicial decisions and opinions. We forget, even the lawyers themselves forget, that it is the lawyers in their offices who make the bulk of our law.

I spent this morning working on a draft of an agreement for the publication of cheap paper-bound books. The signatures of an author and a publisher would turn that agreement into law. This afternoon I watched a client execute a codicil to his will. After he had signed I took the pen. I took it, because it was my own. But if it had been his, he might well have given it to me as a governor might give me the quill with which he had signed a statute which I had drafted. For this codicil was none the less a part of our law. This evening I read the announcement in the afternoon paper of a new bond issue. I recognized one which three of my partners had been working on, drawing the mortgage which secured it and the agreement under which it was to be underwritten and sold. This was law for everyone who bought or sold those bonds.

Where two or three, or more, are gathered together in contract, they set up a small momentary sovereignty of their own. There is nothing fanciful about this. A contract is a little code for a special occasion. A lease is a little statute for your tenancy of a house you have neither built nor bought. Partnership articles or the charter and by-laws of a corporation are quite an elaborate code of law for those who are concerned. A corporate mortgage is a piece of legislation for a large and shifting population of bondholders, affecting, it is true, only a part of their lives, but affecting that part as completely as experienced and foresighted lawyers working late into the urban night can make it. Mark Howe, speaking of the New York Bar, said "as draftsmen of indentures, consolidations, and plans of corporate reorganization they framed constitutions for finance and industry no less important to vast numbers of the people than the national constitution itself. As architects of corporate feudalism their achievements were prodigious." [1] Holmes called a testator, making his will, "a despot, within limits, over his property." [2] It is impossible not to give these private authorities a legislative standing in the law. [3]

This private legislation has something of a life of its own, irrespective of legislatures and courts. For one thing, most of it looks for its enforcement to that posse of social fears, private prides, and economic pressures which we are likely to call good faith, and which is just as powerful as the expectation of compulsion. And the more the lawyer who drafts a document anticipates enforcement by the law, the more he prevents it; and the more it takes the place of law. For the very purpose of the document is to avoid recourse to the courts. In his book about the Cravath firm, one of the oldest and largest of the New York law firms, Robert Swaine says, "A century ago the practice of law was essentially advocacy; it was not until the economic revolution which produced Big Business in the last decades of the 19th Century that the lawyer who devoted most of his efforts to avoiding litigation, rather than conducting it, achieved prominence . . . the modern corporate client expects its business so to be handled as to keep it out of the courts." [4]

This is law which the parties make for their own small domain. As a matter of fact, much of it becomes law for others as well, by imitation. An agreement proves satisfactory. It is not copyrighted. Unlike the latest song, you can copy it for free. It may even get into a law book, and acquire the authority of print, or even of precedent. Other lawyers use it, as we all use any device that saves us time, thought, or the burden of unconventionality. Originality is a vice in this branch of literature. Any substantial change would incur responsibility as well as tempt litigation. Finally it becomes as established in our law as a folk song in our literature, and in strictly the same way. A book of legal forms is the legal cousin of an anthology of popular ballads.

So we have the lawyer as legislator. I tried to get at the lawyer as advocate by way of the ethics of advocacy. I am going to get at the lawyer as legislator by way of the theory of the interpretation and its counterpart, the drafting, of the legislation which, as I say, includes the legal documents which lawyers draft for their clients as well as statutes and administrative regulations.

There are two theories. One is the orthodox theory, which is unsatisfactory, not to say fantastic. It leads the judges up a dead-end street. It does not reflect the actual practice of lawyers. I will state it, and then show you how unsatisfactory it is. The other is a better theory. It opens the way for judges to go as far as they sometimes must go to perform their full judicial function. It explains what lawyers do in fact when they draft a legal document.

The Search for Intention

Lawyers, almost all of them, I think, have been brought up in the belief that the interpretation of legal documents consists essentially in a search for the intention of the author. I take it the classic, and I am sure the most elegant, exposition of this doctrine is a paper which a learned English lawyer named Vaughan Hawkins read before the Judicial Society in London nearly a hundred years ago. In this country there is no better authority than James Bradley Thayer, and he said of Hawkins' paper, "the nature of the inquiry is described with penetration and accuracy." [5]

Hawkins states the lawyers' creed in a few sentences. "In the interpretation of written language in the most general form . . . the object is a single one—to ascertain the meaning or intention of the writer—to discover what were the ideas existing in his mind, which he desired and endeavored to convey to us. . . In the interpretation of a legal document, however, we have not indeed a different, but an additional object of inquiry. We desire not solely to obtain information as to the intention or meaning of the writer or writers, but also to see that that intention or meaning has been expressed in such a way as to give it legal effect and validity; we desire, in short, to know what the writer meant by the language he has used, and also to see that the language used sufficiently expresses that meaning. The legal act, so to speak, is made up of two elements,—an internal and external one: it originates in intention, and is perfected by expression. Intention is the fundamental and necessary basis of the legal effect of the writing; expression is the outward formality annexed by the law. . ." [6]

This is what lawyers were brought up on, and what most of us still believe, or at any rate take for granted. For it is still the orthodox theory of legal interpretation.

The recent Restatement of Property of the American Law Institute says:

"The dominant objective of construing a conveyance is to determine the disposition which the conveyor wanted to make. This depends upon an ascertainment of what may be termed his subjective intent, in so far as he had one. But there are difficulties in ascertaining subjective intent."

The Restatement lists these difficulties, such as inadequate evidence, rules of policy, and continues,

"Hence the judicial ascertainment of the intent of the conveyor is a process which combines an orderly, but somewhat restricted, search for his subjective intent, with supplementing inferences of an intent which the conveyor probably would have had, if he had addressed his mind to those problems which, in fact, have arisen out of his conveyance." [7]

Take Trusts, and *Scott on Trusts* carries as much authority as a Restatement.

"The terms of the trust are determined by the intention of the settlor at the time of the creation of the trust, and not by his subsequent intention. . . The settlor's words or conduct subsequent to the creation of the trust, however, may be admissible in order to show what his intention was at the time of the creation of the trust. . ." [8]

This is enough, more than enough, to show that the familiar doctrine is current as well as orthodox.

This search for the intention of the author is not very old, as things grow old in the law. It is more orthodox than ancient. Wigmore dates its origin around the turn of the eighteenth century into the 1800's.[9] I suppose it must be regarded as one of the reforms of the Enlightenment of the eighteenth century. So Hawkins, two generations later, in 1860, was speaking in a spirit of renovation and reform. He was attacking the earlier doctrine, which was medieval and which was still maintaining the position that every word —in the eyes of the law—had one single and immutable meaning. Legal interpretation was then taxonomic, like the Latin names for flowers. "That lawyer's paradise," Thayer called it, "where all words have a fixed, precisely ascertained meaning." [10]

Listen to an English judge, Brook, J., speaking in 1554:

"The party ought to direct his meaning according to law, and not the law according to his meaning; for if a man should bend the law to the interest of the party, rather than the interest of the party to the law, this would be the way to introduce barbarousness and ignorance and to destroy all learning and diligence. For if a man was assured that whatever words he made use of, his meaning only should be considered, he would be very careless about the choice of his words, and it would be the source of infinite confusion and uncertainty to explain what was his meaning." [11]

And this only ten years before the birth of Shakespeare who made words, including legal words, flow more happily and freely than any man, before or since, has ever succeeded in doing. Medieval doctrines die hard.

As late as 1814, another English judge, LeBlanc, J., called the new inquiry after intention "a very dangerous rule to go by, because it would be to say that the same words should vary in construction." [12] The same thought led Baron Parke, in 1833, to say, "In expounding a will, the Court is to ascertain, not what the testator actually intended, as contradistinguished from what his words express, but what is the meaning of the words he used." [13]

You see how persistent the medieval attitude was, how atavistic the legal mind is. Even in the minds of the best of judges, well into the nineteenth century, the medieval attitude persisted. Indeed, a remnant of it still persists in the doctrine that a "plain meaning" cannot be disturbed.[14] Plain, that is, to lawyers. Even now, the flood of the inquiry into intent has not covered this medieval ledge. If you make what you say too plain to lawyers, too easy for them to understand, they will not listen to anything else.

Not a bad example is the case of a lady who left the residue of her estate to "my heirs at law living at the time of my decease." The lawyer who drew her will asked her, "Who do you want to get the rest of your money? Who are you nearest relatives?" She said, so he testified, "I've got about twenty-five first cousins. Let them share it equally." And her lawyer wrote down, "to my heirs at law living at the time of my decease." She neglected to tell the lawyer that her aunt was still living, and, when the aunt survived her, the aunt became her only heir, as every lawyer knows; and of course took all her money.[15] So long as there was an aunt, it would never have occurred to the judge that "my heirs at law" could mean cousins. Nor had it occurred to the testatrix that she was living in the Middle Ages.

The law is taking such an unconscionable time to rid itself of this medieval illusion that each word has, and can have, only one taxonomic meaning, because the law was stepping out of one illusion into another, which, though more enlightened, was even more illusory, that words in themselves have no meaning at all and that we must look through them and behind them and peer about for what the author intended. This is pure hallucination. Here lawyers are not even looking for a black hat in a dark room. If there is any hat there at all, it is on their own head.

Curiously enough, lawyers recognize this without dismay. Hawkins, unappalled, said,

"It is to be observed, that there may be cases where intention can and must be inferred, although, in fact, there may have been none. The interpreter cannot certainly know whether the intent existed; it is the indicia of intent, the marks or signs which accord reasonable presumption of its existence, which he can alone regard, and these he is bound to regard, although, in spite of such indications, there may have been no actual intention." [16]

It is difficult to infer an intention which as likely as not may not exist. Scott handles the difficulty with circumspection. He falls back, as the *Restatement of Property* did, on Gray's shrewd observation in his *Nature and Sources of the Law*. Citing Gray's book Scott says,

"In many cases the court is ascertaining not what the settlor actually intended in regard to a particular matter but what he would have intended if he had thought about the matter." [17]

Gray was talking about the interpretation of statutes. There, of course, the orthodox theory becomes quite obviously absurd, as so many have pointed out. But no one better than Gray himself:

"A fundamental misconception prevails, and pervades all the books as to the dealing of the courts with statutes. Interpretation is generally spoken of as if its chief function was to discover what the meaning of the Legislature really was. But when a Legislature has had a real intention, one way or another, on a point, it is not once in a hundred times that any doubt arises as to what its intention was. If that were all a judge had to do with a statute, interpretation of statutes, instead of being one of the most difficult of a judge's duties, would be extremely easy. The fact is that the difficulties of so-called interpretation arise when the Legislature has had no meaning at all; when the question which is raised on the statute never occurred to it; then what the judges have to do is, not to determine what the Legislature did mean on a point which was present to its mind, but to guess what it would have intended on a point not present to its mind, if the point had been present." [18]

Learned Hand has made much the same observation. Answering the question, how does the judge in fact proceed?, Hand said, "Although at times he says and believes that he is not doing so, what he really does is to take the language before him, whether it be from a statute or from the decision of a former judge, and try to find out what the government, or his predecessor, would have done, if the case before him had been before them. He calls this finding the intent of the statute or of the doctrine. This is often not really true. The men who used the language did not have any intent at all about the case that has come up; it had not occurred to their minds. Strictly speaking, it is impossible to know what they would have said about it, if it had. All they have done is to write down certain words which they mean to apply generally to situations of that kind." [19]

Or, to take what Hand said nearly twenty years later, in 1952, "The issue involves the baffling question which comes up so often in the interpretation of all kinds of writings: how far is it proper to read the words out of their literal meaning in order to realize their overriding purpose? It is idle to add to the acres of paper and streams of ink that have been devoted to the discussion. When we ask what Congress 'intended,' usually there can be no answer, if what we mean is what any person or group of persons actually had in mind. Flinch as we may, what we do, and must do, is to project ourselves, as best we can, into the position of those who uttered the words, and to impute to them how they would have dealt with the concrete occasion. He who supposes that he can be certain of the result is the least fitted for the attempt." [20]

It is somewhat surprising to find the Supreme Court canonizing Gray's analysis of "what the judges have to do" and Hand's what a judge "really does" and "must do" into a judicial duty to do it. The smile with which Gray so often wrote as well as talked would have burst into a laugh if he had seen his "have to" turned into an "ought to," and Hand must have joined him when his statement of fact was transmuted into legal doctrine. Yet this is just what the Court did in the case of *Vermilya-Brown Co. v. Connell.*[21] It was a matter of applying the Fair Labor Standards Act to Bermuda after we had leased it as a military base in 1940.

The Act, which was passed in 1938, covered "any territory or *possession* of the United States" as well as the United States themselves. I emphasize the key word. Two years later, and quite unexpectedly to Congress, we leased part of Bermuda from Great Britain as a military base. Did the Act apply to employees of contractors working on the base? "The point of statutory construction for our determination is as to whether the word 'possession,' used by Congress to bound the geographical coverage of the Fair Labor Standards Act, fixes the limits of the Act's scope so as to include the Bermuda base." Yes, said the Court, five of them, over the vehement dissent of Jackson, Chief Justice Vinson, Frankfurter, and Burton.

There is no reason why we should discuss the propriety or the wisdom of the United States in treating a military base which it had leased from Great Britain as one of its "possessions." The Court was the only responsible agency that was in favor of doing so. The Department of Justice filed a brief against it. The State Department officially deplored it. The Wage-Hour Administrator ruled against it. Jackson said, in his dissent, "Such a decision by this Court initiates a philosophy of annexation and establishes a psychological accretion to our possessions at the expense of our lessors, not unlikely to be received in more critical quarters abroad or confirmation of the suspicion that commitments made by our Executive are

lightly repudiated by another branch of our Government. It should
be the scrupulous concern of every branch of our Government not
to overreach any commitment or limitation to which any branch
has agreed."

What had led the majority seemingly so far astray? They were
no less scrupulous and no more imperialistic than the other branches
of our Government. The trouble was they thought it was their duty,
their judicial duty, to guess, not at what Congress would do, but
what Congress would then have done, if Congress had foreseen the
pickle the Court was in now. "Under such circumstances, our duty
as a Court is to construe the word 'possession' as our judgment in-
structs us the lawmakers, within constitutional limits, would have
done had they acted at the time of the legislation with the present
situation in mind." It puts a great strain on a man's wisdom to feel
he is under the duty of making up his own mind only by filling
it with what another did not have in his.

The doctrine is not only absurd, but a bit sinister. One man's
guess is another man's prejudice. Take another equally egregious
example of the operation of the orthodox theory on the interpretation of a statute. The statutes of Massachusetts have for generations
provided that "a person qualified to vote for representatives to the
General Court shall be liable to serve as a juror."[22] Then in 1920
by the Nineteenth Amendment women became just that, "qualified
to vote." The Amendment said, "The right of citizens of the United
States to vote shall not be denied or abridged by the United States
or by any state on account of sex." Did that bring women into the
category of persons liable to serve as a juror?

True, the Chief Justice said, "the word 'person' when used in an
unrestricted sense includes a woman." Indeed, he added, it may include even a national bank or a corporation. Yes, but—

"It is clear beyond peradventure that the words of G.L. Ch. 234,
sec 1, when originally enacted, could not by any possibility have
included or been intended by the General Court to include women
among those liable to jury duty." "Manifestly, therefore, the intent
of the Legislature must have been, in using the word 'person' in
statutes concerning jurors and jury lists, to confine its meaning to
men."

But the Nineteenth Amendment? "The Nineteenth Amendment

to the Federal Constitution conferred the suffrage upon an entirely new class of human beings. . . No member of the class thus added to the body of voters had ever theretofore in this Commonwealth had the right to vote for candidates for offices created by the Constitution."

The Chief Justice was no feminist. "The change in the legal status of women wrought by the Nineteenth Amendment was radical, drastic and unprecedented. While it is to be given full effect in its field, it is not to be extended by implication. It is unthinkable that those who first framed and selected the words for the statute now embodied in G.L. Ch. 234, sec. 1, had any design that it should ever include women within its scope. It is equally inconceivable that those who from time to time have reenacted that statute had any such design. When they used the word 'person' in connection with those qualified to vote for members of the more numerous branch of the General Court, to describe those liable to jury service, no one contemplated the possibility of women becoming so qualified."

Certainly not. "The conclusion is irresistible that, according to sound principles of statutory construction, it can not rightly be held that the scope of R.L. c. 176, sec. 1, the statute in force on August 26, 1920, now G.L. 234, sec. 1, was extended by the ratification of the Nineteenth Amendment so as to render women liable to jury duty. To reach that result would be directly contrary to every purpose and intent of the General Court in enacting that law." [23]

Perhaps this is more silly than sinister, that a word large enough to have space for national banks and corporations had no vacancies for women. I cannot help wondering what the Court would have done with a stiff property qualification for voters after it had been likewise later repealed. But this is the orthodox doctrine. Orthodox, but not universal. Of course it has been criticized and repudiated. Frankfurter, in the course of his Cardozo Lecture before the Association of the Bar of the City of New York in June, 1947, said, "You may have observed that I have not yet used the word 'intention.' All these years I have avoided speaking of the 'legislative intent' and I shall continue to be on my guard against using it." [24]

The courts used to be fastidious as to where they looked for the legislative intention. They used to confine the inquiry to the reports by committees and statements by the member in charge of the bill.

But now the pressure of the orthodox doctrine has sent them fumbling about in the ashcans of the legislative process for the shoddiest unenacted shreds and patches of intention.

This is a little hard on the legal profession, and it is a wonder that the bar does not complain. That it has not complained, shows how deeply embedded the doctrine is in the legal mind. Jackson has pointed out the practical consequences to the profession, "The custom of remaking statutes to fit their histories has gone so far that a formal Act, read three times and voted on by Congress and approved by the President, is no longer a safe basis on which a lawyer may advise his client, or a lower court may decide a case. This has very practical consequences to the profession. The lawyer must consult all of the committee reports on the bill, and on all its antecedents, and all that its supporters and opponents said in debate, and then predict what part of the conflicting views will likely appeal to a majority of the Court. Only the lawyers of the capital or the most prosperous offices in the large cities can have all the necessary legislative material available. The average law office cannot afford to collect, house and index all this material. Its use by the Court puts knowledge of the law practically out of reach of all except the Government and a few law offices." [25]

Back in 1857, Congress provided that no testimony given by a witness before a Congressional committee "shall be used as evidence in any criminal proceeding against him in any court, except in a prosecution for perjury committed in giving such testimony." [26] *Any* court? The Supreme Court of Maryland protested that this did not mean a Maryland trial court, because it was a *state* court. So the objections of one Adams, who had been convicted of running a gambling business, to the use of his testimony before a Senate Committee were overruled. The Supreme Court of the United States set aside his conviction. "Any court" meant any court. Jackson concurred, but he wanted to emphasize something. It was this,

"What someone intended almost a century ago when it was passed, or in the 1890's when Counselman v. Hitchcock, 142 US 547, was decided, I do not know. Since the last event, some thirty Congresses have come and gone, something near 15,000 Congressmen have been elected, not allowing for reelection. How many of them knew of Counselman v. Hitchcock, how many felt frustrated by it, and how many would have vented their frustration by repeal, I do not know or care. Congress left the Act on the books, and it was there when this petitioner testified. The only question is what it would mean to a reasonably well-informed lawyer reading it. . .

". . . A lawyer would be warranted from the face of this Act in advising the witness that he had nothing to fear from frank and complete disclosure to Congress. Thus the Act would have accomplished its obvious purpose of facilitating disclosure." [27]

The doctrine has had a natural, but surely an unintended, consequence on legislation. It gives anyone who drafts an act, committee members, and its counsel, the administrative agency involved, even lobbyists, a right, anyhow the opportunity, to plant expressions of intention for the very purpose of having the courts nose them out and use them. Archibald Cox says, "It is becoming increasingly common to manufacture 'legislative history' during the course of legislation. The accusations of outside participation made in Congress, and the elaborate interpretations in some passages in the committee reports, suggest the danger that this occurred during consideration of the Taft-Hartley amendments." [28]

When Congress, or any legislature, enacts a statute, it expresses itself in certain words, and in nothing else. It knows that those words will come up for interpretation by the courts, because the legislature knows they will have to apply its words to particular cases on particular occasions. The real intention of the legislature is that the courts shall interpret these words in the immediate presence of a particular occasion. It may have hopes. It may have expectations. But they are unenacted. They are not law. However wise a legislature may be, however foresighted, even prophetical, yet it is dealing in nothing more than foresight. A legislature is dealing exclusively with what may happen, and so cannot possibly go into the details. The courts, on the other hand, are at grips with what did happen or with what is happening, and so they have all the details before them. The courts would, therefore, do better to pay the legislatures the true courtesy of recognizing what is expected of them, and what only they are in a position to do, than to wish their judicial problems back on a legislative committee whose function is only advisory or on a member whose function is only argumentative. Let the courts stop peering over the shoulders of legislative committees and sitting in the strangers' gallery. The Congressional Record is not the United States Code.

Why shouldn't the judges accept the responsibility which the legislature has given them and do their best to fulfill it? If the judges do it acceptably, so much the better. If not, the legislature will always have the last word. If the courts put a bulge in the phrase, or a dent in it, the legislature can always straighten it out. Anyhow, this would be an admirable way of inviting the legislature's attention to improvements. Learned Hand wrote to Brandeis, "There are wrongs which in fact legislatures cannot be brought to take an interest in, at least not until the Courts have acted." [29] It is hard to believe that any harm would come of the courts' acting on the real facts of their function and of their relation to the legislature instead of paying the false courtesy of bowing to something that is not there. The only possible relevance of a past intention is the likelihood that it still exists. The only rational reason why the courts should ask what the legislature did intend is the likelihood that it still does.

The courts would be better occupied trying to foresee what the present legislature, or the next legislature, will do than to divine what some past legislature would have done. The legislature which passed the statute has adjourned. Its members have gone home to their constituents, some of them, or all of them, to a long rest from all lawmaking. Why bother about how they would have decided the present case? The courts had better be prophetic than archaic, they had better pay a decent respect to the present, or to a future legislature, than stand in awe of one that has folded up its papers and joined its friends at the country club, or the lodge, or in the cemetery. Better that the courts set their decisions up against the possibility of correction by their immediate masters than set them in the shadow of the past. Historical research is only an excuse to shirk their judicial responsibilities in the inescapable present. Better obey your teacher than your grandfather.

There are lawyers who will call this crude, that the courts would do better to try to anticipate the wishes of their present and future masters than divine the past intentions of their predecessors. It seems crude, but only because lawyers prefer the past to the future. They are more likely to be historically than prophetically minded.

Yet if a court were to deliberate on what the present or a future legislature may do, after it had read the court's opinion, after the court had explained the situation, after the court had exhibited the whole fabric of the present law into which this particular piece of legislation must be fitted and adjusted, then the legislature would be legislating, as it should, in the light of the current of the whole of the law, instead of being instructed only about one obsolete bit of it.

None of the judges, so far as I know, has taken this attitude toward Congress or any legislature, but some of them have taken it toward the Supreme Court, and a higher court can and does tell off the lower courts with quite as much force and with the same effect as Congress can tell off all the courts. Some of the judges have been looking to what they think the Supreme Court will tell them to do instead of what it did once tell them. Listen to Judge Learned Hand. It is always hard, and here it is impossible, not to quote him.

"It is always embarrassing," Hand wrote, "for a lower court to say whether the time has come to disregard decisions of a higher court, not yet explicitly overruled, because they parallel others in which the higher court has expressed a contrary view. I agree that one should not wait for formal retraction in the face of changes plainly foreshadowed; the higher court may not entertain an appeal in the case before the lower court, or the parties may not choose to appeal. In either event the actual decision will be one which the judges do not believe to be that which the higher court would make. . . Nor is it desirable for a lower court to embrace the exhilarating opportunity of anticipating a doctrine which may be in the womb of time, but whose birth is distant; on the contrary I conceive that the measure of its duty is to divine, as best it can, what would be the event of an appeal in the case before it." [30]

Judge Peter Woodbury took the same line in one of those cases where citizenship had been denied to a man who was not willing to bear arms in war. Three times the Supreme Court had denied citizenship, but in each case only by a small majority. [31] Judge Woodbury's court followed the three decisions, but he dissented, saying, "I would probably feel compelled to follow them, were it not for my view that now the Supreme Court itself would not do so . . . I believe that the prediction can be ventured that the above cases are no longer expressive of the law. And I believe that this prediction can be ventured even resisting the temptation 'to embrace the exhilarating opportunity of anticipating a doctrine which may be in the womb of time, but whose birth is distant.' Therefore, I feel that we are not constrained to follow the Supreme Court cases cited last above." Judge Woodbury was proved right, for the Supreme Court did indeed itself refuse to follow them and granted the man citizenship.[32]

Even in Contracts?

Come now to contracts. Here the hunt for the Snark runs into a further difficulty. Not only what we are looking for may not be there, but each party may quite justifiably have a different intention, so justifiably that there may even be no agreement of minds, and so no contract at all. The doctrine requires us to search for a joint intention, an intention which is shared by all the parties and which they did not see fit, or did not dare, to express. The Restatement of Contracts prudently refuses to lay down any rule. Instead it lists half a dozen standards of interpretation: general usage, which shades off, of course, into one of any number of special usages, local or occupational or other; the mutual standard of what both parties actually intended; the individual standard of what each actually intended; a standard of reasonable expectation, that is, the meaning which a party should reasonably have apprehended that his words would convey to the other; and a standard of reasonable understanding, or the meaning which the person to whom the words are addressed might reasonably give them. We are thrown into the same state of mild confusion as we are when the waiter hands us the menu.

Williston undertakes to explain all this, and to help us to choose. I will go briefly into his explanation, only far enough to give Williston's own choice.

"It is useless to talk of the 'meaning' of a contract or agreement unless it is known whose meaning is sought; and this inquiry cannot be disposed of by the answer—the meaning of the parties. The inadequacy of such an answer is obvious. The parties may not have had the same intention. Furthermore, the courts, after asserting that what they are seeking is the intention of the parties, generally add that this intention can be proved only by what they say and do.

In other words, it is not the intention of the parties that is material, but the meaning that the court gives to their manifestations."

He comes to the conclusion that "The standard most applicable to a bilateral transaction would seem to be that of reasonable expectation, No. 5, that is, the sense in which the party using the words should reasonably have apprehended that they would be understood by the other party."[33]

Though Williston regards this as in theory the right standard for all contracts, he goes on to say that the law imposes a different standard where the contract is in writing and the law requires that its meaning be discovered exclusively in that writing, as under the Statute of Frauds or the parol evidence rule. There, Williston says, the standard must be "the ordinary meaning of the writing to parties of the kind who contracted at the time and place where the contract was made, and with such circumstances as surrounded its making." This is, of course, the special usage of the locality, occupation, etc., No. 2 of the Restatement, as Williston says in a footnote.[34]

It is clear that Williston takes no interest in the hunt. For him the meaning of a contract is to be sought in your reasonable expectations of what meaning the other party will give to your words; or, when the policy of the law requires you to put them down in writing, they must be intelligible enough to be understood by such people as share your circumstances. Both are objective standards; and, as Williston says, only in two cases do they reach different results. One, of course, is where there is such a justifiable difference in meaning that the parties do not meet in any contract at all. In the other, considerations of policy interfere and hold the parties down to ordinary usage. Here the law does not leave the parties free to attach their own private meaning to words which in public ordinarily bear another. You will detect a slight odor of the medieval about legal policy here. At least I do. But scarcely enough to be musty.

Holmes was another who took no interest in the hunt for intention. In a short article he referred to Hawkins, disagreed with him, and went on to say,

"It is not true that in practice (and I know no reason why theory should disagree with the facts) a given word or even a given collection of words has one meaning and no other. A word generally has several meanings, even in the dictionary. You have to consider the sentence in which it stands to decide which of those meanings it bears in the particular case, and very likely will see that it then has a shade of significance more refined than any given in the word-book. . .

"How is it when you admit evidence of circumstances and read the document in the light of them? Is this trying to discover the particular intent of the individual, to get into his mind and to bend what he said to what he wanted? No one would contend that such a process should be carried very far, but, as it seems to me, we do not take a step in that direction. It is not a question of tact in drawing a line. We are after a different thing. What happens is this: Even the whole document is found to have a certain play in the joints when its words are translated into things by parol evidence, as they have to be. It does not disclose one meaning conclusively according to the laws of language. Thereupon we ask: not what this man meant, but what those words would mean in the mouth of a normal speaker of English, using them in the circumstances in which they were used, and it is to the end of answering this last question that we let in evidence as to what the circumstances were. But the normal speaker of English is merely a special variety, a literary form, so to speak, of our old friend the prudent man. He is external to the particular writer, and a reference to him as the criterion is simply another instance of the externality of the law." [35]

Holmes, then, would apply to all contracts the standard or rule which Williston says the law imposes on those which it requires to be in writing. They are both offering us a laicized version of the medieval theory. Instead of a fixed and immutable meaning which the law assigns to each word, they are offering us the sense in which a reasonable layman in the given circumstances would assign to it. A layman in the circumstances when the words were uttered takes the place of the lawyer in court or in consultation. This is all to the good, and better by a long shot than what the medieval law prescribed for us, but there is no reason why we should forget that it is essentially no more than a new model of the old theory.

This is what Holmes and Williston would substitute for the

orthodox illusion that we can turn interpretation into an inquiry after a subjective intention. I think we can do better, and I can now state my thesis very easily. Holmes's insistence on the external standard of the normal speaker and Williston's belief that the other party has something to do with meaning point the way I am taking. This is not to say that I agree with either Holmes or with Williston, but that will become clear as I go on.

The Virtue of Vagueness

Of course words can and do have many meanings. Even a whole document has a certain play in the joints, as Holmes said, when its words are translated into things. I want to go farther and assert that all words which are applicable to things, even in the particular context of the circumstances in which they are uttered, with the exception only of proper names and singular terms which purport to name one and only one object—an exception which I will discuss later when I come to wills—always have many meanings. Their author, I say, expects them to, wants them to, indeed uses and even comes to admire this above all their other virtues. So, I say, we are not talking about one meaning, as both Holmes and Williston were, neither the meaning which their author intended, nor the meaning which a reasonable person would ascribe to them, nor the meaning which either party expected of the other. We are all of us, the author, the person to whom they are addressed, the court, and therefore you and I too, we are all dealing with sets or groups of meanings; and by meanings I mean particularly applications. I don't know what else this word signifies.

These words—I include, of course, phrases and sentences and complete documents—have size as well as color and quality and, having size, they contain within themselves groups of meanings. It is this comparatively drab and uninteresting quality with which we are concerned in legal interpretation. Have you ever watched a lawyer drafting a legal document for you? Only a good poet manipulates words at once more tenderly and more ruthlessly, but a poet sees and uses all their characteristics, their color, their texture, their luster, all their virtues. The legal draftsman works only in black and white, in browns and grays, in high lights and in shadows, in a chiaroscuro of clarity and obscurity. He is concerned with the size of the words he uses, their shape and contour. He works in only two of their dimensions, so to speak. These words include a number of particular applications, some more, some less. A word can be adjusted, by the addition of adjectives and qualifying phrases, to cover less, or a word can be selected for its size. Words and phrases can be either adjusted to or selected for, the required size and shape. This, essentially, is the craft of the draftsman.

This is the virtue in words which the good draftsman learns to use, and in the end, admire. It is a quality which has been too much and too long neglected, perhaps because people who love words have been more interested in literature than in law, and this quality is too drab to excite them. They have given their attention to the abstract and the concrete. Lawyers are concerned with the general and the particular.

The distinction is as significant as it is subtle. I was at first misled into ignoring it by not being able to see any difference between the concrete and the particular. But the other ends of the two sticks are far apart. Let me transpose what Quine has said into what lawyers have to deal with. We talk about negligence or about fraud. These are abstract terms. They name a property which is shared by those acts which we call negligent or fraudulent. These are general terms, not abstract. They are synonymous, you say. No, the act is not the same thing as one of its properties, as lawyers should know better than others. For lawyers, in their practice, deal with the acts themselves.[36] "Men, not Man: people, not the People: Hands: mouths: arms: eyes: not syllables," as MacLeish says.[37] A lawyer does not have a case of fraud or a case of negligence. He is presented with and he is engaged to deal with certain particular acts and events—so particular in many ways they are unique—which someone has called negligent or fraudulent in one aspect.

You ask, reasonably enough, what the difference is, what odds it makes which he calls them. Quine says that as soon as we elevate general terms to the status of singular abstract terms, as we do when we think in terms of "negligence" instead of "negligent acts," we run into the question whether there are any such abstract entities. Quine wants to keep logic and logicians clear of this metaphysical question. The consequences for lawyers are more serious. Lawyers' careers are devoted to particular events. When they start thinking that they are dealing only with the properties of those events, they lose touch, they take their eyes off the ball, they start making gestures. They could not do worse.

The verbal virtue which resides in general terms has not been wholly neglected. Vaughan Hawkins quotes the great German scholar Savigny as saying that "the excellence of a Roman law lay in its being neither too plain nor too obscure, but expressed in a sort of middling obscurity, *'auf einem schmalen Raume mittelmäs- siger Dunkelheit.'* " Hawkins does not agree at all. He hastily adds that this "sounds ironical, and is manifestly appropriate only to writings which, like Roman laws, and perhaps the saying of some philosophers, are made avowedly with a view to being interpreted, and not to legal writings in general, which, it will be admitted on all hands, *ought* to be so plain as not to require interpretation." [38] No, what they ought to be is as plain and precise or as ambiguous and imprecise as a good draftsman sees fit to make them.

The virtue which resides in the size of words has been as much of a commonplace among logicians as the search for their author's intention among lawyers. Logicians call it the extensive meaning of words, as distinguished from the intensive. Jevons explains the distinction neatly in *Elementary Lessons in Logic*,[39] published more than ten years after Hawkins. As that is too long to quote here, let me quote one of the best of our contemporary logicians. C. I. Lewis says that of "the two modes of meaning" which are "traditional and familiar, though not always specified in the same way, the denota- tion or extension of a term is . . . the class of all actual or existent things which the term correctly applies to our names." [40]

The intensive meaning of a term, on the other hand, is a quality which we have ascribed to everything in the class, which we have abstracted from each of them. It is an undue interest in the intensive meaning, and an emphasis upon it alone, which have led lawyers into the paper chase for abstractions which they call intentions. For abstractions have the appearance of being precise, and lawyers cherish a prejudice in favor of precision, however illusory, just as Hawkins did. Impreciseness and vagueness have been regarded as defects and not as another natural characteristic of words.[41]

The extensive meaning of a word, Lewis says, is "the class of all actual or existent things which the term *correctly* applies to." But the area of a word is seldom or never staked out with enough precision to enable the class to be "correctly" enumerated or defined. Its boundaries are vague and penumbral. Or, to put the same thing another way, "correctly" calls for a decision by someone. Take almost any word, legal or not, and you will readily think of a number of particular applications to which it may or may not apply. The law books are full of them. Indeed I doubt if you can find any case in the books which does not raise just such a question.

All this is obvious enough, once we have got over our prejudice for the precise, and are willing to recognize the equally admirable properties of selective and adjustable inexactitude. Then we shall be free to substitute for what the orthodox theory of interpretation calls the intention of the legislature, of the party to the contract, of the grantor, of the testator, the particular thing to which the word is applied by the person, whoever it may be, to whom the words were addressed and to whom the power of applying them was delegated. The vaguer they are, the more imprecise they are, the greater the delegation. Inside, well on the inside, of the area of their meaning there will be little or no doubt or obscurity or even disagreement. But along the margin, in the skirts of the forest, there will be doubts of the correctness of the application. Here lies controversy and litigation, in which the question must be decided; but the question is not whether the doubted, denied, controverted, and now litigated application is or is not to be taken as what the word means, but whether the person to whom the word was addressed acted reasonably in choosing and acting on the one of many meanings on which he chose to act. It is not simply what would a reasonable man have taken the words to mean, or what the speaker would reasonably have expected him to understand. If we make this the meaning, we are committed to the fallacy of the single right meaning. There is a world of difference between what a reasonable man would have done and whether a particular man acted reasonably. Did the conduct of this person unduly stretch the tether of this word? This is the question, and thus the problem of interpreting legal documents becomes one with an old and familiar problem in the law, the question of reasonable conduct. The courts can then handle the interpretation of documents like any other of a man's acts.

It is fair to ask what criteria I should expect the courts to apply when they come to answer this question, whether the addressee has acted reasonably, whether he has abused his discretion, whether he has exceeded his authority, or however you want to put the question which would be presented to the courts. An equally fair answer would call for a book, perhaps nothing short of a great book on jurisprudence, or a greater book on what is Justice. I am not going to try to say what Justice is, except that she is not a solemn maiden sitting blindfolded, holding scales which she can only pretend to read. About the criteria which the courts should apply, all I can say is that they transcend the author's intention, however well discovered and demonstrated. For recourse to his intention is not simply an oversimplification of the problem and therefore a restriction of the criteria to one factor in the great equation of Justice. It is an escape from the problems of the present into the happy hunting country of the past.

The grave fault of the orthodox theory is that it assumes that the author retains control over his words after he has uttered them. How can he? He knows that his words are to be applied by others in the future, by others over whom he may have no control except by litigation, and in a future in which he may have no part. The orthodox theory is no more than a futile gesture of maintaining his control over his words by expecting everyone to surmise what he may have meant by them.

The author of a legal document is trying to control the future. You and your lawyer are not just trying to express yourselves. This, to be sure, is a part of the picture, but only a very small part. The orthodox theory has been nearsighted, and by peering exclusively at this very small and unimportant part of the picture it has stultified itself, instead of standing back and admiring the whole picture of what you and your lawyer were trying to do. "How futile it is," Alan Gardiner says, "to describe the purpose of speech as the expression of thought." Speech, he claims, is used "in order to influence the conduct of others." [42]

You are trying to influence the conduct of the people to whom the document is addressed. You are trying to lay hands on the future, to control their conduct in the future. You want to assure yourself, so far as you wisely can, that six months hence, two years hence, or if it's a will you are making, at some undetermined time hence, this or that will be brought to pass, that someone, your partner if it's articles of partnership, or the purchaser of your property, if it's a deed, or your executor, if it's a will, or all of us, if it's a statute, will behave in a certain prescribed way. You are trying to stabilize a part of the future, set it on a course, make it more foreseeable and more reliable. Legal draftsmen must stop thinking of themselves as creative writers—to use a pretentious phrase—or even ghost writers. Lawyers may be artists in other peoples' troubles, but when it comes to writing, they are only artisans. And our courts are critics, not historical societies reading papers at us, or the judges, when they dissent, at each other.

There are other ways in which words can be used to control the future behavior of people than by legal documents. Eloquence, persuasion, indeed fraud and deceit, offer their own methods, but they are best served by argument, forensic or domestic, by appeals to our emotion, by abuse of our confidence. I am not talking about them. I am talking about the interpretation of legal documents, from promissory notes to statutes and constitutions. Their way of affecting or controlling the future is the legal way, and it is based upon the liabilities, penalties, and sanctions which the law imposes, though it may call in a posse of private shames and social stigmas. And all of these are contingent upon whether the future conduct is or is not described in these legal documents. It is, therefore, only a question whether certain future behavior, certain future acts and events, fall within or without the scope of the words which the legal draftsman is selecting for your client. The problem before him is the matching of words with future events. But what happens in the future is necessarily uncertain, inchoate, contingent, only partly foreseeable, and he must, therefore, find some similar and corresponding quality in the words he is using. Briefly, his words should be as flexible, as elastic, indeed as vague, as the future is uncertain and unpredictable. I say *vague,* because both *flexible* and *elastic* imply sharp edges and definite contours. A lawyer's words should be no more precise than his client's control of the future is both practicable and desirable.

So the meaning of words is to be sought, not in their author, but in the person addressed: in the other party to the contract; not in the grantor but in the grantee; not in the testator but in the executor or the legatee; in the defendant who is charged with violating the statute, in the conduct of any person who is acting under the authority and either within or without the authority of the words to be interpreted. Words are but delegations of the right to interpret them, in the first instance by the person addressed, in the second and ultimate instance by the courts who determine whether the person addressed has interpreted them within the scope and extent of their authority.

What the courts have to decide, then, is whether the addressee has applied or proposes to apply the words within the authority they have given him. I do not see how the courts can very well succeed until they recognize that this is what they are doing. Surely what is sought has something to do with the search. At the end of "The Theory of Legal Interpretation," Holmes says, "Although practical men generally prefer to leave their major premises inarticulate, yet even for practical purposes theory generally turns out the most important thing in the end." [43]

I have shown that the theory I offer you is based on a natural virtue in words themselves. Let me state this theory of interpretation dogmatically before I turn the coin over to show that it conforms with the actual practices of draftsmanship.

Words in legal documents—I am not now talking about anything else—are simply delegations to others of authority to apply them to particular things or occasions. The only meaning of the word meaning, as I am using it, is an application to the particular. And the more imprecise the words are, the greater is the delegation, simply because then they can be applied or not to more particulars. This is the only important feature of words in legal draftsmanship or interpretation.

They mean, therefore, not what their author intended them to mean, or even what meaning he intended, or expected, reasonably or not, others to give them. They mean, in the first instance, what the person to whom they are addressed makes them mean. Their meaning is whatever occasion or thing he may apply them to or what in some cases he may only propose to apply them to. The meaning of words in legal documents is to be sought, not in their author or authors, the parties to a contract, the testator, or the legislature, but in the acts or the behavior with which the person addressed undertakes to match them. This is the beginning of their meaning.

In the second instance, but only secondarily, a legal document is also addressed to the courts. This is a further delegation, and a delegation of a different authority, to decide, not what the word means, but whether the immediate addressee had authority to make them mean what he did make them mean, or what he proposes to make them mean. In other words, the question before the court is not whether he gave the words the right meaning, but whether or not the words authorized the meaning he gave them.

In appropriate cases, to be sure, the law allows the person to whom the words were addressed, their immediate addressee, to ask the court a different question—not the extent of his authority, but simply what he ought to do. This is a little unusual, for usually a court is required only to pass judgment upon a man's conduct, whether he has done what was legal or whether he has acted reasonably, or less often, whether he is going to. Usually a court looks at a man's predicament from the outside. It is somewhat exceptional to require a court to put itself in the man's place, substitute itself for him. But here, in these cases, a man is given the right to ask the court's advice, so to speak. He is acting under the authority of a document upon which he must rely, but which he is not sure how to interpret, not sure enough anyhow to ignore what others might take it to mean, who might then charge him with misinterpreting it. He is, let us say, an executor or a trustee, and files a petition for instructions; or he is a stakeholder and files a bill of interpleader. In these and other such cases, he is impartial and indifferent to the result. He does not care what meaning is selected and applied. As Holmes said, "I am much more disposed to regard trustees as a sort of domestic tribunal, *ex necessitate,* between the parties subject to the control of the courts in case of a want of good faith or reasonable judgment." [44]

Nor, of course, does the court care. It wants only to settle the controversy. So the court tries to strike the center. It ignores what other meanings the words may carry, what other conduct they might justify, and seeks the one safest and most generally satisfactory and acceptable meaning, that is, the most obvious meaning. We must not be confused when the court tries to give it the appearance of being the words' only meaning. It is really only an adjudicated best meaning.

In every other, and in the usual, case the legal draftsman must have two things in mind when he selects a word. First he must consider the extent of authority or discretion he is giving to the person to whom in the first instance the word is addressed. At the same time he must keep in mind the question which will be presented to the court if it comes, as it may, to interpret the words. This is, except in those special cases I have just mentioned, whether the person to whom the word was addressed has exceeded its authority or abused the discretion it gave him.

Language, at any rate in legal documents, does not fix meaning. It circumscribes meaning. Legal interpretation is concerned, not with the meaning of words, but only with their boundaries.

Legal Draftsmanship

So much for a theory of interpretation which I believe fits the nature of language better than any other, and most assuredly better than current doctrine. The obverse of the coin is draftsmanship. If I had any judicial authority for this theory, I should cite it and so approach the drafting of legal documents by way of the judicial doctrines which a draftsman must expect will be applied to his work. I have no authority. All I can do, then, is show that this theory fits exactly what the draftsman does in fact do, notwithstanding and in the teeth of the current and mistaken judicial doctrine.

One of the amiable myths of the law is that the bar follows the law. No, the converse more nearly fits the facts. One virtue of the theory of interpretation which I am offering lies in the fact that it makes it easier for the courts to conform to the practice of the bar. I propose, therefore, now, to show by some examples that the bar is right in practice. Good draftsmen will learn little or nothing from what I am going to say. They know it already, though they may not all be fully aware of it.

Take first a form for an unsecured loan agreement. You are the vice-president of a bank. You want your lawyer to put in a provision requiring the borrower to keep its working capital up to some fixed amount. You reject the phrase, "working capital," as a bit too loose. You are not sure that it has enough technical meaning. Instead you ask him to put, "the excess of the total current assets over current liabilities," which has a firmer technical usage. And you make it the firmer by qualifying it, "determined in strict accordance with sound accounting practice." But then you remember that you are requiring annual audit reports by an accountant. So you tell him to add, "by the independent certified accountants responsible for the preparation of the audit report."

Thus you adjust the scope and tether of the discretion you are delegating by adding qualifying words and phrases. For this is what they do. Every word you add modifies the future power of action of the person you address, here a prospective borrower. If you hadn't put in "independent," the borrower might have used its own accounting department. If you hadn't put in "certified" you could not object that he hadn't been certified.

And yet you have respected the fact that times do change, and accounting practices with them. You are dealing with the future and you do not want to tie the borrower down too tight, nor the bank down with him, to present accounting practices. They are to be "sound," but currently, not presently sound. Moreover, within the scope of that word "sound," are left all the discretions which engage so much of the attention of accountants.

Is it not misleading to talk about the bank's intention, or even about what a reasonable man would take these words to mean or what the bank might reasonably expect its client to take them to mean? Your bank does not live in an expressionist world, nor is it dealing with any hypothetical reasonable man, nor with its own reasonable expectations. It is dealing with certain particular individuals who are going to act in their own particular ways, and your client expects just that of them. Within limits as broad and wide as it dares, you and your bank want them to do just that.

Take a separation agreement. You are the husband and you have had to agree that your wife shall have the custody of the children. This is almost plenary discretion. All she will concede is "the right to visit the children at reasonable times and places." In effect she retains the discretion which reposes in that ample phrase, at least in the first instance, because the children will be with her. But you will not stand for that. You want "the right to have the children live with him during the summer," and you demand this further concession. But your wife recognizes that "summer" is a vague word and, though she will be in a position to determine when it starts, how long after Labor Day may you choose to prolong the visit? For you will then have the discretion. So you have to compromise. You agree to wipe out almost all discretion by adding, "which period shall, subject to unavoidable adjustment, begin June 15th and end September 15th of each year." It is a barter of discretions, with neither you nor your wife willing to give the other any more than either has to, and finally trading it out into as little as possible.

Take now a situation where you have almost plenary power to make the discretion as narrow or as broad as you choose. You are bound only by two considerations. You know that you will not be present yourself to supervise what you want done; and at the same time you know that you do not know precisely how it had better be done. At any rate you ought to know this. If you don't, your lawyer must tell you.

As you see, your lawyer is drafting your will. He comes to the powers of the executor or the trustee. He takes up the provision which tells your trustee how to credit receipts and charge payments in his probate accounts. One way would be to copy into your will the definition of net income from the Internal Revenue Code, and add as many of the Regulations as you choose. I do not say it is the best way, or even advisable, although it would go far to reduce the annoying difference between your trustee's probate account and his income tax return. For it would give your life tenant all the breaks. I need not tell you that Congress has taken full advantage of the Sixteenth Amendment. But it would relieve your trustee of a good deal of responsibility, because it would very much narrow his discretion. He would have to give everything to the life tenant.

Parenthetically, let me say that a Congressional Committee drafting a definition of net income stands in the same relation to the Treasury Department, with the same power of giving it much or little discretion, as a testator to the trustee under his will. There is no essential difference between public and private documents so far as the theory of their interpretation is concerned.

But then it occurs to you that after all you are choosing your own trustee and can have confidence in him. So you ask your lawyer to provide only that stock dividends shall be added to principal except when paid in lieu of regular cash dividends, or that bond premiums shall not be amortized, or that depreciation must be handled this way or that. In all other respects you want to leave your trustee free—within the bounds of the words principal and income, as free as the Sixteenth Amendment made Congress.

In your next will you want to make your son executor. There is not even a hesitation of confidence. You want to give your son all the discretion you can. So your lawyer writes, "My executors and trustees shall have power to credit receipts and charge payments to income or to principal or to both as may seem fair to him though not in accordance with the law."

You have given him as much discretion as you can. What is your intention, in the sense the orthodox doctrine gives to that word? Your intention is to have no intention, in that sense anyhow. It is an abdication, not an assertion, of any intention. Your son is to do as he chooses, within the farthest bounds of the words, income and principal, whatever the judges may have said in other cases, and whatever you might have thought.

I see no reason to treat wills as such, or legacies and devises as such, any differently from any other document. In a way, and I think it is the relevant way, wills are little statutes and testators little sovereigns of their small domain. As I have said, Holmes called them "despots, within limits." [45]

I see no reason why wills should be interpreted any differently from statutes, but I recognize that with wills the courts are under a peculiar temptation to administer that kind of justice which consists in satisfying only the immediate parties.

Perhaps then, in dealing with wills, the courts sometimes yield too easily to the temptation of being guided by the author's intention. For a testator carries, or it seems he ought to carry, a prestige which the parties to contracts and what we may call more democratic arrangements do not and cannot aspire to. Courts are tempted to take the easy way of interpretation by playing on that modicum of respect which executors and legatees, and even not too distant heirs, feel for a testator. When the parties to litigation feel this way about anything, the court is under a great temptation to satisfy them and call it a day.

I can make this quite clear by the case of the trust for charitable purposes by a living donor, whenever the donor expresses dissatisfaction with the way his money is being spent. Now any lawyer could tell either of them that it is none of his business. Only the attorney-general through his visitorial powers or the courts with their powers of cy pres have anything to say about how that trust ought to be administered and how that money ought or ought not to be spent. But a living and dissatisfied donor seems to have a right to make a nuisance of himself. Dead donors, who leave no heirs, or anyway only uninterested heirs, are blessed. Living donors who know when their function ceases go to the highest heaven. The intention of the author is always an intruder, and the respect which is paid to his intent is a peg on which the courts often hang a quick convenient form of justice. This, I think, is the only valid reason to treat the interpretation of wills in any way differently from other documents.

A Precise Degree of Imprecision

Any good theory has its own inherent limitations, and so here. This theory of interpretation applies to all general terms. It does not apply to singular terms, those which purport to name one and only one particular object.[46] Singular terms are the limiting case. Lawyers have all been brought up on the case of the devise of "my manor of Dale," when the testator had two, or the legacy of "my watch" when he had two. Four of the five examples which Hawkins gave in the course of his paper are of this kind.

I offer you the case of Mary Jackson, who was an elderly British spinster and who left a fifth of the residue of her estate to "my nephew Arthur Murphy." Three of them showed up. She had two legitimate nephews called Arthur Murphy. One lived in Australia. Another had stayed in England, but his father, Mary's brother, had died, and this Arthur was inheriting the share his father would have taken in Mary's money. There was a third Arthur Murphy who was also her nephew, though he was the illegitimate son of Mary's sister. Mary had always called him her nephew, and he was in fact managing her affairs. And it was he who got the fifth. He was the one, the court said.[47] Pretty plainly he was the one Mary had in mind.

The theory will not work here, because it is based on the extensive meaning of general terms. Here we are dealing with a singular term, and we do not know, yet have to decide, what word or which word the testator or other author used. For we are dealing in these cases with two words, homonyms. They may sound alike. They may be spelled alike and so look alike, but they are only dressed alike. They may be twins, but they are two individuals. So I find it easier to think of them as two different words than as one word with two meanings. You may prefer to call them ambiguous; that is, in the strict sense of ambiguity, which must on no account be confused with generality. Ambiguity must be reserved for terms which have two or more quite separate meanings or applications.

Whether we think of these words as different words or as the same word with different meanings, they are singular terms, words and phrases which purport to apply to one and only one object. They are in effect proper names. Wills offer the usual examples, but not the only ones.

Holmes put the case of the two ships of the same name. "The defendant agreed to buy, and the plaintiff agreed to sell, a cargo of cotton, 'to arrive ex Peerless from Bombay.' There were two such vessels sailing from Bombay, one in October, the other in December. The plaintiff meant the latter, the defendant the former. It was held that the defendant was not bound to accept the cotton." "The true ground of the decision," Holmes said, "was not that each party meant a different thing from the other . . . but that each said a different thing." [48] There was not one name, any more than there was only one ship. As Holmes said, "They are different words." [49] There were two ships and each had its own name, however much they sounded alike on the tongue of the broker, however much they looked alike to the scribe who made a fair copy of the contract, or to the stenographer who in our day would type it out.

In such cases as these, a search for the intention of the author, testator, or party, is both necessary and harmless. The particular application of the word he used is not in question. It is a search for what word was used, not how it could be applied. If we confine inquiry about the author's intention to the case of the singular homonym or the strict ambiguity, we shall keep out of trouble, and leave theory intact.

Names and singular terms mark the extreme exactitude and precision of which words are capable. With them stand those terms which refer to an ascertainable group of objects, two, three, four, or more, with as much exactitude as if there were but one. The phrase, "heirs at law," is a good example. As soon as you state whose heirs you are referring to and the date when they are to be determined and what law is to determine them, you have a precisely ascertainable class. So your lawyer will probably write out, "the person or persons whom and in the shares and proportions in which my administrator would have been required to pay the same had I died intestate and possessed thereof immediately after the termination of such trust," or some other equally elegant circumlocution.

These terms for groups which are as precise as a name or a singular term bring up the difference between general terms and vague terms. Your lawyer has both at his disposal. When he wants a compendious word of the required size, he usually has his choice between a term which quite definitely and precisely covers as much ground as he wants to cover, and a vague term, which is elastic or flexible enough to be stretched over the same ground. As always, it is a choice between making up your mind now or leaving it to someone else to make up his mind for himself later.

Which choice had the Fathers made when they drafted the article in the Constitution on the Judiciary? This was a problem which was put up to the Supreme Court in 1949. The jurisdiction of the federal courts includes suits "between Citizens of different States." Congress had tried to enlarge this jurisdiction to include also suits in which a citizen of a territory or of the District of Columbia was a party. Was the District a "State"? [50] Was the word "State" here in the context of the Third Article a word of a fixed and definite size, which meant no more than those states which had been admitted to the Union? Or was it, on the other hand, vague and flexible enough to be stretched to include the District, as certainly seemed advisable? Frankfurter and Reed thought it could not, just because it seemed clear to them that here in the Third Article the Fathers had chosen a word of a fixed and definite meaning.* They said,

* No one needs to be bothered by the fact that in other places in the Constitution, this word "State" is flexible enough to include the District and the Territories; e.g., in the next paragraph but one, in this same Article Third,

"The precision which characterizes these portions of Article 3 is in striking contrast to the imprecision of so many other provisions of the Constitution dealing with other very vital aspects of government. This was not due to chance or ineptitude on the part of the Framers. The differences in subject-matter account for the drastic differences in treatment. Great concepts like 'Commerce . . . among the several States,' 'due process of law,' 'liberty,' 'property' were purposely left to gather meaning from experience. For they relate to the whole domain of social and economic fact, and the statesmen who founded this Nation knew too well that only a stagnant society remains unchanged. But when the Constitution in turn gives strict definition of power or specific limitations upon it we cannot extend the definition or remove the translation. Precisely because 'it is a *constitution* we are expounding,' we ought not to take liberties with it.

"The very subject matter of sections 1 and 2 of Article 3 is technical in the esteemed sense of that term. These sections do not deal with generalities expanding with experience. Provisions for the organization of courts and their jurisdiction presuppose definiteness and precision of phrasing. These requirements were heeded and met by those who were concerned with framing the Judiciary Article; Wilson and Madison and Morris and Rutledge and Sherman were lawyers of learning and astuteness. The scope of the judicial power with which the federal courts were to be entrusted was, as I have said, one of the most sharply debated and thoroughly canvassed subjects in Independence Hall. When the Framers finally decided to extend the judicial Power to controversies 'between Citizens of different States,' they meant to be restrictive in the use of that term.

---

where the trial of all crimes must be by jury, and in the Sixth Amendment, where they must be speedy and public, the word "State" certainly includes the District and the Territories. A good example of a word making a quick change of personality is the word "person" in the Sherman Act. Within only twelve words, "person does not include the United States (*United States* v. *Cooper*, 312 U.S. 600) and then does include a State (*Georgia* v. *Evans*, 316 U.S. 159). These "conclusions" the court said, "derived not from the literal meaning of the words 'person' and 'corporation,' but from the purpose, the subject matter, the context, and the legislative history of the statute." (*Parker* v. *Brown*, 317 U.S. 341 at 351.) From what else does anything or anyone derive its personality? These may be twins, but they are different persons.

They were not unaware of the fact that outside the States there was the Northwest Territory, and that there was to be a Seat of Government. Considering their responsibility, their professional habits, and their alertness regarding the details of Article 3, the precise enumeration of the heads of jurisdiction made by the Framers ought to preclude the notion that they shared the latitudinarian attitude of Alice in Wonderland toward language." *

Whether Frankfurter and Reed were right about this particular word need not concern us. They were certainly right to protest against the notion that Humpty Dumpty is the patron saint of legal linguistics. It is just as important that legal draftsmen, and specially the draftsmen of a constitution should have precise words at their disposal, words that are fixed and immutable in their precision as it is that the draftsman have in his vocabulary a great gamut of words which are as vague as he chooses, up to words which have scarcely even a personality of their own. For the law is not to be confined in a nutshell. Fair, reasonable, equitable, proper, due, they are all familiar enough, and they are so nearly empty of any but emotional meaning that they express little more than an attitude. They are receptacles to be filled from some future context of circumstance. They are bourns to be achieved as well as believed. The

* Frankfurter's later statement to the same effect to the court in *Rochin* v. *California*, 342 U.S. 165 at 169-170: "In dealing not with the machinery of government but with human rights, the absence of formal exactitude, or want of fixity of meaning, is not an unusual or even regrettable attribute of constitutional provisions. Words being symbols do not speak without a gloss. On the one hand the gloss may be the deposit of history, whereby a term gains technical content. Thus the requirements of the Sixth and Seventh Amendments for trial by jury in the federal courts have a rigid meaning. No changes or chances can alter the content of the verbal symbol of jury—a body of twelve men who must reach a unanimous conclusion if the verdict is to go against the defendant. On the other hand, the gloss of some of the verbal symbols of the Constitution does not give them a fixed technical content. It exacts a continuing process of application.

"When the gloss has thus not been fixed but is a function of the process of judgment, the judgment is bound to fall differently at different times and differently at the same time through different judges. Even more specific provisions, such as the guaranty of freedom of speech and the detailed protection against unreasonable searches and seizures, have inevitably evoked as sharp divisions in this Court as the least specific and most comprehensive protection of liberties, the Due Process Clause."

bad draftsman squanders them. The good draftsman cherishes them, because they allow him to make his immediate meaning as scarce as he chooses. From octave to octave, he puts the person he is addressing into as more or as less of a commanding position as he chooses.

Without such words as liberty, property, and due process of law, which put us, so far as we dare to trust each other, in command of our own fate, we could not have a written constitution. We have gone a long way toward reliance on written words. The farther we have gone, the more we have found it necessary to make them vague. Business could no more do without this cardinal verbal virtue of vagueness than businessmen could afford to lose their basic confidence in one another. If the meaning of legal documents were to be made as precise as lawyers have been brought up to believe it should be, our trade, our commerce, all our affairs, would have to choose between law and living. What we admire in legal draftsmanship is not precision. It is a precisely appropriate degree of imprecision.

Intensive Meanings and Poetry

A theory of interpretation which is grounded on the very nature of language cannot very well stop with the law. Is it as true in literature generally as it is in the law that, as Hobbes says, "a signe is not a signe to him that giveth it, but to him to whom it is made"? [51]

I have said that lawyers work only in black and white, only in chiaroscuro, only in two dimensions, only with the size and the flexibility of words. Poets see and use all their qualities, playing their lights on all their facets. The lawyer is the artisan of extensive meanings. The poet is an artist in intensive meanings.

Perhaps we should try to get away from these two technical terms. The extension of a word is that part of its meaning which is concerned solely with what it refers to, what a singular term refers to and what a general term covers. It is true of those things, and that is all it is. The intensive meaning, on the other hand, is what you and I call meaning, all the rest of the word's meaning. The intensive meaning is the side of the medallion with the head and the superscription on it. The other side is the extensive meaning. It is blank, and only its size is of any interest.

If I drop the metaphor, I can go a little farther. These two meanings determine each other. If we could know the whole extension of a word, we should then know its intensive meaning; and vice versa, if we could thoroughly know its intensive meaning, we'd know its extension. Each, theoretically, would fix the other. But practically, of course, we can never know the whole of either. You can no more know all the things, past, present, and to come, which a word may refer to than the ten-volume Oxford Dictionary can tell you all that a word means. But practice does not lag so far behind theory as to make theory useless. For what we do know about the meaning of a word certainly helps us toward deciding whether its extension covers a given object, and a good way toward understanding what a word means is to run over the things we are sure its extensive meaning includes. This is the very process of generalization.

There are these two aspects of meaning, but there is no reason to think that the relations between the author and the reader do not remain the same, and this is what I want now to demonstrate.

In *Insight and Outlook*, Arthur Koestler three times repeats a passage from Mallarmé which I shall translate:

"I think," said Mallarmé, "there must be allusion. The contemplation of objects, the image which soars up from the reveries which they excite, this is song, this is poetry. The Parnassians exhibit the whole of the object all at once, and make no mystery of it. Thereby they deprive our minds of the delicious pleasure of sharing in the creating. Naming an object suppresses three-quarters of the enjoyment of a poem about it, which consists in the pleasure of divining it little by little. It is the perfect use of mystery that constitutes the symbol: evoke an object little by little in order to show a state of mind, or inversely choose an object and then disengage a state of mind by gradually unveiling it." [52]

Koestler concludes, "The artist's aim is to turn his audience into accomplices . . . it is based on a shared secret." [53] Right, though I do not see the need of clandestinity. The point is, the poet knows he cannot do it alone. Poetry is not soliloquy. An author knows he will give the reader more only by getting him to do more, to take a larger share in the creation. Take a good simple example such as Aldous Huxley gives in *After Many a Summer Dies the Swan*. "Words merely remind you of your memories of similar experiences. *Notus calor* is what Virgil says when he's talking about the sensations experienced by Vulcan in the embraces of Venus. Familiar heat. No attempt at description or analysis; no effort to get any kind of verbal equivalence to the facts. Just a reminder. But that reminder is enough to make the passage one of the most voluptuous affairs in Latin poetry. Virgil left the work to his readers. And, by and large, that's what most erotic writers are content to do. The few who try to do the work themselves have to flounder about with metaphors and similes and analogies. You know the sort of stuff: fire, whirlwinds, heaven, darts." [54]

Of course a poet must not go too far and demand too much of his reader. When Max Eastman protested that James Joyce's *Finnegan's Wake* demanded too much of the reader, Joyce replied, "The demand that I make of my reader is that he should devote his whole life to reading my works." [55] But the more a poet gets out of us, the more he has given us. The more he elicits, the more he has said. There are books you read for what you can get out of them. There are others you read for what they can get out of you. But I ask you if the poet's success does not depend quite simply upon the amount of collaboration he can persuade his readers to give him. His job is to evoke as much as he can, and express as little as he dare. So he ventures into the implicit and allusive. This is what Goethe must have meant when he said that all lyrical work should, as a whole, be intelligible, but in some particulars a little unintelligible.[56]

And Learned Hand has said the same thing about the law. "Law has always been unintelligible, and I might say that perhaps it ought to be. And I will tell you why, because I don't want to deal in paradoxes. It ought to be unintelligible because it ought to be in words—and words are utterly inadequate to deal with the fantastically multiform occasions which come up in human life." [57] I should say, and I don't think paradoxically, that it is simply because our power to understand is greater than our power to express or explain.

Reading and writing are much more nearly the same thing than we generally think. We make the mistake of trying to separate them. Edmund Wilson says that "there is really no way of considering a book independently of one's special sensations in reading it on a particular occasion. In this as in everything else one must allow for a certain relativity. In a sense, one can never read the book that the author originally wrote, and one can never read the same book twice." [58] Let me fortify Wilson with Pascal and Holmes. Pascal said, "It's not in Montaigne, but in me, that I find what I see there." [59] And Holmes wrote to Laski, "The literature of the past is a bore. When it is not so, it is because it is an object of present reflection and scientific study and the interest is in your thought about it, not in it." [60] Fred Allen found TV "too graphic. In radio, even a moron could visualize things his way. . . It was a custom-made suit. Television is a ready-made suit. Everyone has to wear the same . . ." [61]

The author need not ask for our collaboration, nor even be aware of it. Montaigne speaks of "the graces and beauties which are there, not only unintended by the author, but he is not even aware of them. An adequate reader often discovers in the writings of others perfections which the author neither put there nor perceived, and which give us richer aspects and meanings." [62] Proust went further. He said, "Fine books are written in a strange sort of language. Under each word, each of us puts his own meaning, which is often a wrong meaning. But in fine books, all wrong meanings are fine." [63] Proust's word is *contresens*.

One more quotation, which I owe to Kant, via Ernst Cassirer and Edmond Cahn. "It is by no means unusual," Kant said, "upon comparing the thoughts which an author has expressed in regard to his subject . . . to find that we understand him better than he understood himself. As he has not sufficiently determined his concept, he has sometimes spoken, or even thought, in opposition to his own intention." [64]

I quite agree, but can we say that we understand the author better than he understood himself? Is that not his business? I should prefer to say that we understand ourselves better than he understood us, which is our business. Anyhow, as Cahn writes me, what author ever does sufficiently determine his own concept?

There is a fine example of such a *contresens* in the last line of

Ben Jonson's song, "Drink to Me Only With Thine Eyes." William Empson points out that the last line says just the opposite of what Jonson meant, "But might I of Jove's nectar sup, I would not change for thine." "I would *not* change for thine!" Isn't the lady to understand that he *would* prefer her nectar?

Empson suggests a number of implausible explanations, and then comments: "All this may be true, and these facts very interesting to the biographer, but they have nothing to do with the enjoyment of the poem. Of course, such a distinction is hard to draw, and those who enjoy poems must in part be biographers, but this extreme example may serve to make clear that it is not all significant ambiguities which are relevant, that I am talking less about the minds of poets than about the mode of action of poetry.

"This seems an important point, because I am treating the act of communication as something very extraordinary, so that the next step would be to lose faith in it altogether. It might seem more reasonable, when dealing with obscure alternatives of syntax, to abandon the claim that you are explaining a thing communicated, to say either that you are showing what happened in the author's mind (this should interest the biographer) or what was likely to happen in a reader's mind (this should interest the poet). This might be more tidy, but, like many forms of doubt, it would itself claim to know too much; the rules as to what is conveyable are so much more mysterious even than the rules governing the effects of ambiguity, whether on the reader or the author, that it is better to talk about both parties at once, and be thankful if what you say is true about either." [65]

Communication is collaboration. The measure of successful expression, and the mark of good poetry, is the degree of collaboration which the poet can obtain from his readers. It is the function of the critics to help us collaborate with the necromancer who arouses one of our dead selves, touches one of our erogenous spots, and stirs us into a surprised response. We collaborate. What we don't do, and can't do, is put ourselves in the author's place. Nor do we want to. Some of us enjoy Keats, or Shelley, or Byron. But how? In our own way, not in their way.

"In the small dining-room, most of the furnishings came from the Pavilion at Brighton. Four gilded dragons supported the red lacquered table and two more served as caryatids on either side of a chimney piece in the same material. It was the Regency's dream of the Gorgeous East. The kind of thing, Jeremy reflected, as he sat down on his scarlet and gold chair, the kind of thing that the word 'Cathay' would have conjured up in Keats's mind, for example, or Shelley's, or Lord Byron's—just as that charming Leda by Etty, over there, next to the Fra Angelico Annunciation, was an accurate embodiment of their fancies on the subject of pagan mythology; was an authentic illustration (he chuckled inwardly at the thought) to the Odes to Psyche and the Grecian Urn, to 'Endymion' and 'Prometheus Unbound.' An age's habits of thought and feeling and imagination are shared by all who live and work within that age— by all, from the journeyman up to the genius. Regency is always Regency, whether you take your sample from the top of the basket or from the bottom. In 1820, the man who shut his eyes and tried to visualize magic casements opening on the foam of faery seas would see—what? The turrets of Brighton Pavilion." [66]

So it seems to me clear that poets and other authors require as much from their readers as the lawyer, drafting his legal documents, chooses to leave to the persons to whom they are addressed; and, I think, it is more in both cases than either is willing to recognize or admit. A legal document, as we have seen, deputizes as well as decides. So likewise a poem elicits as well as expresses its meaning. The sign is to him to whom it is made. [67]

The Trial Court

The Judge and the Society of Jobbists

We have left the lawyer's office and are on our way to court, the trial court. It is hard to say what is the important thing about the trial court, the one feature which best explains it. The court is the referee of the bouts which punctuate the adversary process toward justice. But that's not it. The court is the critic of our legal linguistics, but even a semanticist must admit that life is more than words, and he won't need a lawyer to tell him that justice is as large as life. So that's not it.

The judicial function has no such particular and distinctive feature as the vicarious nature of advocacy. The judge is not acting for anybody, not even for the state or the government. We expect him to be as independent of the government as he is of any other organization or individual. We no more want him to be corrupted by intimidation than we like to see him bribed. Nor is the judge acting for himself. The worst judicial offense, indelible and unpardonable, would be for him to conduct the trial and render judgment according to his own light, according to his own personal opinion, however devoutly or sincerely held. A judge must take complete leave of himself, his own personality, and his own dearest beliefs. We expect him to be completely detached, not only from others but from himself, and devoted only to his job.

The highest compliment you can pay a judge is to say that he belongs to the Society of Jobbists. This is a society which Holmes founded early in his career, and he became its first president. But he left little written about the Society.[1] Learned Hand is its second president, and here is his description of it. He wrote this before his election, and you must ignore his deplorable false modesty. Otherwise, I believe this is an accurate statement. At any rate, it is the best account we have of the Society of Jobbists.

"Are you a member of the Society of Jobbists, or do you know the guild? If not, let me tell you of it. All may join, though few can qualify. Its president is a certain white-haired gentleman, with a keen blue eye, and a dangerous turn for dialectic. But the other members need not and do not fear him, if they keep the rules, and these are very simple. It is an honest craft, which gives good measure for its wages, and undertakes only those jobs which the members can do in proper workmanlike fashion, which of course means no more than that they must like them. Its work is very various and indeed it could scarcely survive in these days, if the better known unions got wind of it, for quarrels over jurisdiction are odious to it. It demands right quality, better than the market will pass, and perhaps it is not quite as insistent as it should be upon standards of living, measured by radios and motor-cars and steam-heat. But the working hours are rigorously controlled, because for five days alone will it labor, and the other two are all the members' own.* These belong to them to do with what they will, be it respectable or not; they are nobody's business, not even that of the most prying moralists.

"I confess that I have often applied for admission and have been always rejected, though I still live in hope. The membership is not large, at least in America, for it is not regarded with favor, or even with confidence, by those who live in chronic moral exaltation, whom the ills of this world make ever restive, who must be always fretting for some cure; who cannot while away an hour in aimless talk, or find distraction for the eye, or feel agitation in the presence of fair women. Its members have no program of regeneration; they are averse to propaganda; they do not organize; they do not agitate; they decline to worship any Sacred Cows, American or Russian. But none the less, you must be careful how you thwart them. They are capable of mischief; for you must not suppose, because they are amiable and gay and pleasure-loving, because they are not always

---

* This in 1930. In 1925, the members got only a half holiday on Saturday, as we know from a letter which President Holmes wrote to Wu on March 26ᵗʰ of that year.

reverent, that they are not aware of the silences, or that they do not suppose themselves to have embarked upon a serious enterprise when they began to breathe. You may go so far with them in amity and fellowship; you may talk with them till the cocks crow, and differ as you like and as you can, but do not interfere with the job, and do not ask for quarter if you do—you will not get it. For at bottom they have as much faith as you, and more, for it is open-eyed and does not wince. They have looked in most of the accessible closets, and though many are too dark to explore and they know little about what is in them, still they have found a good many skeletons, taken them apart, and put them together. So far as they have got, they are not afraid of them, and they hope that those they have not seen may not be worse than the few they have." [2]

You see it is a guild. As lawyers alleviate the burden and temper the dangers of their necessarily vicarious career by craftmanship, the best judges, when they are working, are nothing but craftsmen. But this does not help us at all to understand what their craft or their job is. So this isn't it.

I don't think I shall be far off the mark if I take the trial court to be a miniature and microcosm of society, enough of a sample and exemplar of ourselves to reflect our current conscience. This, at any rate, is half the story, and a good half to emphasize. For it has been neglected. Lawyers have ignored it, naturally enough. They have have been brought up in the shade of the other, the legal side. Lay-men, I think, have either taken it for granted or they have refused to believe that the law could have such a sunny aspect. Yet the law requires a good court to have what I may call, if you will let me use the word in a technical sense, a popular as well as a legal side. The light by which a good judge, sometimes with the help of a jury, illuminates a case is reflected from us as well as refracted through the technicalities of the law. It is as important that we be our own judge as it is important that we do not act as our own attorney.

The General and the Particular

We sometimes think, we even get used to thinking, that facts consist simply in what happened, what somebody did, what the circumstances were. Pure fact, if you like. This leads us to think of a trial as the reconstruction of such facts followed by their comparison with what should have been done or should have happened; in brief, a description compared with a prescription. This is too simple and mostly mistaken. The reconstruction of the past will, of course, often raise issues of what did indeed happen or what was indeed done, but it is seldom that such pure facts can be challenged and disputed with enough hope of success to pay the price of boring the court. When this can be done and the issue is crucial, the conflict may be very dramatic. This drama darkens our understanding of the usual issues, which are quite different.

The trial courts are more usually concerned with conflicting characterizations of the facts than with the facts themselves. Truth is only a part of justice. "The relevance of a fact in a man's life does not depend on how true it is, but on how significant it is," [3] Goethe told Eckermann, explaining why he called his autobiography, *Dichtung und Wahrheit,* Fiction and Truth. It is not truth that gives significance, or even understanding, to a fact.

Two characterizations or versions of the same facts are competing for acceptance by the trial court. They are rival claims which are put in the form of characterizations or versions of what happened. These versions of fact, much more than the facts themselves, are what the judicial process is dealing with. It is not the application of one kind of thing called law upon another kind of thing called fact. The bulk of a trial court's business is the choosing between two things of the same kind, the parties' conflicting and competing versions of what they can't deny. If you insist on separating law and fact, the best you can do is say that they are different aspects of these versions. A version or characterization of what happened is both law and fact, law when you look at it judicially, fact when you look at it testimonially.

Was a certain course of conduct *negligent?* Was what you said *defamatory?*

What is the right version of the fact that a man or a group holds a certain number of shares in a corporation? How close knit is the group? How large is the next smaller block? How few other holders could make up a larger block, and what is the likelihood that they will? The facts and figures are plain enough, but the question which will worry the court is whether it constituted *control* of the corporation.

Are you a *resident* of this state? Where you voted, or where you slept most of the year, are not the questions which will give the judge pause or keep the jury from agreeing.

Were you *drunk*? Or did you drive so as to *endanger* the lives of others? The answer to these questions is not so much a report of your physical condition or of your conduct as the prosecuting attorney's version of it, his way of putting it. You will not agree that they can be disposed of simply by testimony of how many drinks you had or how fast you were driving.

Whether your wife *deserted* you is a matter of more precision than whether you were guilty of *extreme cruelty*, but something more than a bare recital of the naked truth is required before the judge can call her leaving you a *desertion*, and much more before he can call your conduct *cruelty*.

I have italicized the words which raise the questions we put up to a trial court. As you see, they are versions of what happened, not what happened. Each has its own greater or less degree of generality; and the more general it is, the more of a demand it makes upon the judicial process, for the more it relies for its meaning upon the particular circumstances of the case.

Not only do different words stand at different points on the scale of generality and particularity. The same word in the mouth of a witness is more particular, because it is nearer a particular occasion, than when it reaches the ear of the judge or the jury; and much more particular than when it is later read by a court of appeal. As a word passes from the witness through the trial court, into a written record, and so up to another court, it becomes more and more general, because it is farther removed from a particular occasion. This is in the very nature of the use of words. It is not peculiar to their use in the law. Bertrand Russell has brought this out and, I think, makes it very clear. "Sensation, perception, and memory are essentially pre-verbal experiences; we may suppose that they are not so very different in animals from what they are in ourselves. When we come to knowledge expressed in words, we seem inevitably to lose something of the particularity of the experience that we seek to describe, since all words classify. But here there is an important point that needs to be emphasized: although, in a sense, words classify, the person who uses them need not be doing so. A child learns to respond to stimuli of a certain kind by the word 'cat'; this is a causal law, analogous to the fact that a match responds to a certain kind of stimulus by lighting. But the match is not classifying the stimulus as 'ignitory,' and the child need not realize that the use of such a word as 'cat' does not *presuppose* classification. No one can utter twice a given instance of the word 'cat'; the classifying of the various instances of the word is a process exactly analogous to that of classifying animals as instances of a species. In fact, therefore, classification is later than the beginnings of language." [4]

Facts, Words, and Subtle Minds

The trial judge is working as close as he can to the particularity and subtlety of experience, and yet he works at two removes. One remove, of course, is the witness. The other is the fact that the judge is on the other side of the words. To the witness, as Russell says, the words he is using express as best he can the particularity of his experience. To the judge, the same words can be no more than characterizations or versions of what happened. This is the difference between a judge on the bench and an umpire who speaks with the added authority of a witness. He is leaning over the play as well as passing judgment on it.

This is as it should be, as well as it must be. The word is on its way to a farther removal from actuality for presentation to another judge who sits on appeal and who will take it and treat it as an even more general term which classifies the original experience. If the same word were not susceptible of a more general as well as a more particular meaning, we should have to use two different words, and this would completely sever the law from actual life. As it is, we don't have to translate one word into another. The word itself is translated from one level of generality to another.

The judicial process is a funnel down which a general term becomes particular. Two things need to be emphasized. One is that a generality does not become particular of itself. There is nothing automatic about it. "General propositions do not decide concrete cases." The other is that very often the process is too complicated to be put into words. As Holmes went on to say, "The decision will depend on a judgment or intuition more subtle than any articulate major premise." [5] "Many honest and sensible judgments," he said later, "express an intuition of experience which outruns analysis and sums up many unnamed and tangled impressions,—impressions which may lie beneath consciousness without losing their worth." [6]

With one hand a judge grasps the general words of the statute or of the document. With his other hand he fingers the facts. A good trial judge must have green fingers. Or make it golf instead of gardening. A trial judge is playing a game in which he has to keep his eyes on the ball. He may look down the fairway of the law, take his stance on the statute, waggle the right iron of the leading case, and practice a couple of swings on dicta, but then he must look down at the ball. The better his stance and the better his swing, so much the better his direction and distance down the precedents, but he will not make a good decision unless he keeps his eyes on the instant case.

The trial court has a prodigious task. Lawyers oversimplify it and make it look easier than it is when they try to find some inherent and essential difference between law and fact, and talk about applying the law to the facts.

This, like any other attempt to make a sharp distinction of kind between things which are different in degree, succeeds only by leaving a great gap between facts and law. Facts are reduced to the pure facts of circumstance and brute behavior. Law is reduced to the more precise generalities which lawyers can understand and apply to the brute facts with relative ease. "It is only to the lawyer that the law and fact offer themselves as opposing categories, and this distinction in the lawyer's mind reduces itself to a distinction between what he ought to know as a lawyer and the facts of which a lawyer has no peculiar knowledge. To the learned lawyer, and especially to the really learned judge, law is a part of himself, a part of his actual thought and existence. The thought of my nearest friend is to me a fact, while my own is something more than that, it is my experience and my life. In this way his law presents itself to one who is really learned in it. Such a man solving a legal problem presented to him does not say, such and such a solution seems reasonable or reaches a practical result: he says, it is law. To a learned judge, argument of counsel is not instruction. It does not purport or attempt to tell him what he does not already know. Argument recalls, stimulates, or corrects in a judge his own line of thought. A sound judge in deciding a case does not consciously exercise his will to reach a new interpretation or a new development of law. He merely follows out his own line of thought as a lawyer and registers the conclusion to which he is led as a lawyer by this line of thought. Law, to a lawyer is a part of his own mind; and it is only thus that it differs from fact." [7]

But the law is expected to deal with a number of things which under this definition, the lawyer-like mind, is incompetent to handle. One of them is negligence, a staple in the trial courts. What does the law know about negligence? Nothing, almost nothing, only what is too obvious to argue about. So obvious that the over-eager plaintiff's case is dismissed on his own evidence. "Take, for example, a collision between two motor-cars. There is no way of saying beforehand exactly what each driver should do or should not, until all the circumstances of the particular case are known. The law leaves this open with the vague command to each that he shall be careful. What being careful means, it does not try to say; it leaves that to the judge, who happens in this case to be a jury of twelve persons, untrained in the law. That is a case where the appeal is almost entirely to the conscience of the tribunal." [8]

Or take libel. What is a defamatory statement? Here is the best definition the law can give. "A communication is defamatory if it tends so to harm the reputation of another as to lower him in the estimation of the community or to deter third persons from associating or dealing with him." This is the *Restatement of Torts,* as good an authority as there is.[9] Ask your lawyer whether something you've written is defamatory. He can't tell you. He'll advise you either to take a chance, or spoil what you've written and play safe; or else, if he can, he'll make you fix it so no one can be identified.

Listen to Chief Justice Goddard charging the jury in Harold Laski's libel suit in 1945. "'After all, the truth of the matter is very simple when stripped of all ornaments of speech, and a man of plain common sense may easily understand it; it is neither more nor less than this, that a man may publish any thing which twelve of his countrymen think is not blameable. . . This, in plain common sense, is the substance of all that has been said upon the subject.'" [10]

Or, as Learned Hand put it, "the verdict of the jury is not the conclusion of a syllogism of which they are to find only the minor

premises, but really a small bit of legislation ad hoc, like the standard of care." [11]

"The explanation is plain," Holmes said. "It is that the court, not
entertaining any clear views of public policy applicable to the matter, derives the rule to be applied from daily experience, as it has
been agreed that the great body of the law of tort has been derived.
But the court further feels that it is not itself possessed of sufficient
practical experience to lay down the rule intelligently. It conceives
that twelve men taken from the practical part of the community
can aid its judgment. Therefore, it aids its conscience by taking the
opinion of the jury." [12]

Before we turn to the jury, I want to offer you a long quotation
from Pascal on the difference between *l'esprit de geometrie* and
l'esprit de finesse. This is not so far a cry as it seems. I am going to
translate *l'esprit de geometrie*, by which Pascal meant mathematics
in general, as the legal mind, and *l'esprit de finesse* into the subtle
mind. I think you will then see how apposite and illuminating this
long quotation is. "In the legal mind, the principles are obvious,
but they are not in common use. They stand apart and to one side.
Unless you are practiced in them, it is not easy to turn your head,
they are in plain sight, almost too large to escape you. You must
reason badly to reach a false conclusion.

"In the subtle mind, the principles are common and in plain sight
of everybody. There is no need of turning your head, or of straining
yourself, to see them. All you need is good sight. But your sight
must be good, for the principles are subtle and numerous, and it is
all but impossible that some of them will not escape you. Your sight
must be very keen indeed to see all of them, or your mind exceedingly sound not to reason falsely from only those you do see.

"All legal minds would, then, be subtle if their sight was good,
for lawyers do not reason falsely from known principles; and subtle
minds would be legal, if they could but bend their sight toward
the unaccustomed principles of the law.

"What keeps some subtle minds from being legal is the fact that
they cannot quite turn their heads toward legal principles. What
keeps lawyers from becoming subtle is that they do not see what is
before them. Being accustomed to the large clear principles of the
law and being accustomed to reason only from principles which
they familiarly handle, they are lost in the subleties of principles

which refuse to be handled and which can be even seen only with difficulty. You are more aware of them than you perceive them, and only with infinite pains can you make others aware of them who are not themselves already aware of them.

"For these subtle principles are so delicate and so numerous that your sense must be at once delicate and distinct to be aware of them. And your judgment needs be both correct and sound, where it is seldom possible to prove your principles one by one, as you can in the law. For these are not such principles as you can take possession of. That would be an infinite business. This is a business you must take all at one time, all with one look, and not by a progress of reasoning, not at any rate beyond a certain point.

"So it is rare that legal minds are subtle or that subtle minds are legal, because lawyers want to treat subtle things legally; and thereby they make themselves ridiculous, trying to start from definitions and proceed upon principles, which is not the way in this sort of reasoning. Here the mind works tacitly, naturally, and untechnically. Here no man can express himself, and only a few are even aware of what they are doing.

"The subtle mind, on the other hand, since it is accustomed to passing judgment at one look, is taken aback when it is presented with principles it does not understand; and when it has to start from sterile definitions and from principles it is not used to, and look at them one by one, the subtle mind is repelled and disgusted.

"Minds which work falsely are, of course, neither lawyer-like nor subtle.

"Lawyers who are only lawyers keep, then, their reasoning straight provided everything is explained to them by definition and by principle. Otherwise their conclusions are false and unsupportable, for lawyers are right only when they proceed on clear principles. And subtle minds which are only subtle lack the patience to get down to first principles in anything of a speculative or conceptual nature, things they have never observed and which lie quite to one side of the world they are accustomed to."[13]

The Jury and Your Society

My uncle used to say that the jury served the great purpose of ridding the neighborhood of its sons of bitches. Men have been convicted even of murder in a jury's exercise of this function, but the penalty does not often run so high. The same peculiar trait is imputed to insurance companies, to banks, and to complacent corporations in civil cases; and sometimes the law's ideally reasonable and prudent man, whom a defendant in a negligence case must try to emulate, shares the same imputation. Likewise a jury will often protect virtue against the consequences of a stumble. Many an acquittal, many a judgment for the defendant, is wrapped up in an admonition to go and sin no more. A good physician treats the patients as well as the disease.[14] "Don't forget, George," Jung said to one of his pupils, "medicines cure diseases, but only doctors cure patients." So also the jury sits in judgment on the offender as well as on the offense.

My uncle was undoubtedly right in thinking that the jury often, and not always unjustifiably, confuses what a man is with what a man does. Pascal was saying no more than what my uncle made so clear. For a jury is dealing with matters which must be taken all at one time, all with one look, and not by a progress of reasoning. The term, son of a bitch, is not susceptible of definition. Of all general terms, its meaning is perhaps the most elusive and subtle, and its correct application the most difficult. It is the kind of thing Dorothy Emmet, borrowing from Professor Stocks, calls a "total assertion." [15]

"The distinction between a judgment of faith and a judgment of probabilities may be further elucidated in terms of a distinction drawn by the late Professor Stocks between 'total' and 'partial' assertions. A partial assertion is either a proposition stating matter of fact, verifiable in sense experience, or a logical proposition which can be brought into a coherent system with other logical propositions of the same type. So we could make a number of partial assertions about a man, *e.g.*, that he is bald, aged 55, keeps chickens, is an A.R.P. warden, etc. But if we say that he is a *good* man, we are making a total assertion which cannot be exhaustively analysed into any number of partial assertions of matters of fact. If we were asked why we think he is a good man, we might say that he looks after his old parents, gives away some of his eggs, spends his spare time on A.R.P., and the like. But it might be possible to make any number of partial assertions of this kind, and yet they would not mean the same as we mean when we say that so-and-so is a 'good' man. For it might be possible to enumerate a whole series of estimable acts, and ways of behaving, and yet at the end of it all we might not be willing to say that so-and-so was a 'good' man. ('Though I bestow all my goods to feed the poor, and though I give my body to be burned, and have not charity, it profiteth nothing.' To say someone 'has charity,' as distinct from doing charitable acts, would appear to be a total judgment of his character, like saying that someone is good.)" [16]

Doctors do this, treat the patient as the unit, and lawyers too know that clients come into their offices as often as cases. But if the law should take the individual as the unit and not what he did, there is an end to the rights of individuals. To be sure, the law cannot ignore the fact that it is an individual who is guilty of the crime he is charged with, or liable for the course of conduct which is complained of; but the unit which the law deals with must, so far as possible, be his particular act, not the individual himself. It is what he did, not what he is, that is come to judgment. The law must do its best to regard him as irrelevant, and therefore free. The difference is as vast as the difference between the liberty of a man to be himself and his liberty to do what he did. But my uncle was right. Juries are likely to treat the individual as a unit, just as doctors and lawyers find they have to. So too must the law. The law cannot listen only to partial assertions, to speak in Miss Emmet's language, and be wholly deaf to what she calls total assertions. This is a great problem in the law, perhaps the greatest, so far as our individual liberties are concerned.[17] With doctors and lawyers we solve it by hiring and firing them, by making them our servants. Only in their service is our perfect freedom. The law extricates itself by calling in a jury and by identifying it, so far as it can, with ourselves.

The right to be tried by a jury is the home of our liberties. This is as true as it is trite. It is a facet of the fact that our liberties live only in ourselves. They are inalienable because if we try to alienate them they vanish.

The jury has other functions, as my uncle would have agreed. Jurors are observers, to see how the judicial process works and how the judges behave. It is our way of insisting that citizens visit the courts from time to time and report to each other on the administra-

tion of justice. Otherwise all we should know about it would be
from litigants, lawyers, and newspaper reporters. It is the one
official way, other than voting, that a citizen, simply as such, can
take part in our government.

The jury has the function of making exceptions. We are rule-
ridden. Juries relieve the judge of the embarrassment of making
the necessary exceptions. They do this, it is true, by violating their
oaths, but this, I think, is better than tempting the judge to violate
his oath of office. Thus the law may ignore necessary exceptions to
its necessarily strict rules, much a miracle allows the order of
nature to proceed on its orderly way, indifferent and unaffected,
intent on the next event.

This, of course, is as illogical as it is disingenuous in such a completely logical system as the law undertakes to be. Logically an
exception to any rule can be only the intrusion of another rule.
"Thou shalt not kill" has obvious exceptions, not only in battle but
at the bedside, for example, as some argue, a mother must die in
order to save the child. Such so-called exceptions are dictated by
other rules, which we profess to recognize, but which are usually
so hard to express that they are impossible to apply. Practically,
however, and ignoring pretentions to logic, there are exceptions,
and the law looks to the jury to make them, because the law does
not feel able to make intelligible enough rules to cover them; or
perhaps because the law reluctantly admits that it is less than a
complete logical system.

Euthanasia is one example of exceptional cases. The law recognizes that it is incapable of dealing with euthanasia directly and
candidly. So the law handles these killings deviously, or better,
disingenuously. Lacking itself the genius to cope with them, the law
turns them over to a jury, puts the jury on oath to decide according
to the evidence, and at the same time takes pains to set no penalty
on the jurors if they break their oaths. Thus the law denies to its
right hand what its left hand is doing. Not since the seventeenth
century has the jury's oath to "well and truly try the issue between
the commonwealth and the defendant according to your evidence,
'So help you God'" been enforced. Not since 1670, when a jury
was imprisoned for acquitting the Quaker William Penn. *In
memoriam* Chief Justice Vaughan, who released this jury on habeas

corpus after another judge had sent them to jail for not following his instructions on the law.*

This disingenuous course is surely wiser than a hopeless attempt to discriminate in statutory language those occasions when a daughter or a doctor had better kill her father or his patient. It is wiser than it would be to leave the decision to experts, who are bounded in a nutshell just because they don't have bad dreams, for bad dreams are what anyone who has to decide such a question ought to have. Experts are the last people to trust here. It is wiser too, I think, though surely more devious, than leaving the jury wholly free. If the circumstances are so compelling that the defendant ought to violate the law, then they are compelling enough for the jury to violate their oaths. The law does well to declare these homicides unlawful. It does equally well to put no more than the sanction of an oath in the way of an acquittal. There is, it seems to me, a nice, and a useful, difference between an oath with a penalty and an oath without one. When the half gods go—after all the law is only half divine.

It is the jury's function to evoke and apply the other rules which lie behind these exceptions. For these tacit patterns of behavior are as truly law for the jury as the statutes and precedents which are law to the judge. But they are equally truly law to the judge who is sitting without a jury. This is the usual phrase, "sitting without a jury." It mistakes, at any rate it underrates, the judge's function when he is trying a case alone. It would be better to say that he is sitting instead of a jury or as if he were a jury. Judge Wyzanski reports, "Indeed I have heard federal judges confess that in a Fed-

---

* Bushell's Case, Vaughan 135. See William S. Holdsworth, *History of English Law* (London, 1903), vol. 1, p. 345. It is well to remember that in earlier days in America a jury was not violating its oath by coming in with a verdict contrary to the law laid down by the judge. See Mark Howe, "Juries as Judges of Criminal Law," *Harvard Law Review* (1939), vol. 52, p. 582. In 1808 there was a dramatic case in Massachusetts in which the leader of the bar insisted on arguing the unconstitutionality of an Act of Congress, the Embargo Act, to the jury, in the face of the judge's threat to commit him for contempt. He was not committed and he won his case. This was Samuel Dexter. See Charles Warren, *The Supreme Court in United States History* (Boston: Little, Brown, 1937), Vol. I, p. 342. See also my paper before the Massachusetts Historical Society in 1954.

eral Tort Claims Act case they try to make their judgments correspond with what they believe a jury would do in a private case." [18]

I cannot say this would be so in all kinds of cases. There are cases in which the jury is out of place. At least there are cases in which a jury's peculiar talents are inappropriate. Such are those where the issues are mainly commercial or financial. But in libel, slander, false arrest, fraud, deceit, and negligence, and in divorce cases where adultery is the issue, and in all but trivial criminal cases, the jury is more sensitive and more perspicacious than all but the most talented and understanding of judges.[19] Here the best thing a good judge can do is emulate a jury.

Nor can I say that the law wholly agrees with me. The law insists on making it hard for the judge to act like a jury by requiring him to make specific findings of fact instead of giving a general judgment one way or the other. This makes the judge's decision less final and conclusive, because specific findings of fact are in effect reasons for his conclusion, and so open it up to discussion and make it more vulnerable to argument. Moreover, a court of appeal is reviewing the judgment of a man who has had similar training and who has a similar attitude toward life. The appellate judges are more familiar with the way a judge's mind works. So they may have more respect, but they have certainly less awe than they have for the relatively unknown and mysterious working of a jury.

However, sitting alone without a jury, or, as I say, instead of a jury, a judge must be a man as well as a lawyer, unlearn and yet not wholly forget all the law has taught him. His sight must be very keen, as Pascal said, to see all the subtleties with which he is here dealing. He must be something like what Sancho Panza was to Don Quixote. "The basis of his personality is that sound empirical common sense, that spontaneous wisdom which goes in England by the name of mother-wit. This natural gift is wont to be almost infallible when exercised on the concrete, positive and tangible facts of everyday life. . . But once he gets away from the concrete, the man of sound common sense, for lack of the light of abstract reason, wanders like a blind man burdened rather than helped by his store of experience. Such is Sancho, perfectly described in a suggestive Spanish phrase: 'a sack of truths,' i.e., truths without organic co-ordination, loose like stones in a sack. This is the inner significance of the strings of proverbs, in season and out, which Sancho threads into his speeches, as Don Quixote himself suggests when he calls him 'nothing but a sackful of proverbs and sly remarks.' " [20]

The jury is the way the law extricates itself when we insist that it solve problems which it knows are beyond its own competence. When the general terms of the law are too far removed for the lawyer-like mind to mediate between them and the immediate occasion, the law, like Pilate, and equally prudently, washes its hands and asks the jury to see to it.

Consider the way jurors are selected and the way juries are required to sit and act in judgment. Then tell me if the jury does not seem to have been fashioned for this very purpose. Its form, I say, is functional.

Juries are made up on the basis of the exclusion of the unfit or inconvenient, not selected for skill or experience. Each state has its own qualifications, and the federal courts are more likely to pick and choose than county officials, but by and large a citizen is qualified for jury duty, if he is not too young and not too old, neither infirm nor decrepit, if he has not been convicted of serious crime, if he can read and write English; and is not a soldier or sailor, doctor or dentist, pharmacist or embalmer, policeman or fireman, newspaperman or lawyer, for their services may be insistently and unexpectedly needed elsewhere.

A list of such men and women is drawn up, excluding those who have served at all recently, and they are called up by lot. A panel of them then appear in court at the appointed day and from them each particular jury is drawn, again by lot. Then comes another sifting. The judge excuses those who ask to be excused, when they can show cause, say kinship, interest in the case, prejudice, and so forth. If you are called and want to be excused, you must stand up and give the judge a good reason, or you may smile and nod to one of the lawyers and the other lawyer will challenge you. For each litigant has a right to challenge and exclude a certain number without giving his reason.

The jurymen have never worked together before, probably never even known each other. The jury is a company of strangers, to each other, to the judge, to the parties. They come to their duties

as fresh and as inexperienced as possible and into the case as ig-
norant of what it is all about as they are of the law. The jury is an
ancient and traditional institution, but each jury is no more of an
institution than a few weeks worth of tradition can make it.

No group, of course, can be just a number of individuals. When
two or three, or twelve, are gathered together in the name of anything, something arises in the midst of them. In a religious group
the catalysis is quicker. Dr. Holmes referred in *Elsie Venner* to the
"devotional contact which makes a worshipping throng as different
from the same numbers praying apart as a bed of coals is from a
trail of scattered cinders." [21] In danger, the process is even quicker,
but any serious purpose, even simply a singleness of function, given
time, will do the trick, and the requirement of unanimity in a
jury's verdict may hasten the process. There is no doubt that sometimes a jury soon becomes more than twelve individuals. I have
known of one jury whose foreman happened to be a clergyman
and he led his little group in prayer every morning before they
filed into court. But the law does what it decently can to keep
solidarity as well as curiosity out of the jury room.

There are two or three things about the procedure which these
twelve individuals are required to follow which likewise show how
painstakingly the law ushers their deliberations and their decision
along the subtle intuitive way. In the first place, they are expected
to take all the evidence visually and orally. As little as possible is
given them in writing. There are the exhibits, to be sure, and they
go with the jury when it retires. But no note taking. At any rate
this is discouraged. Picture yourself sitting on a long case. Wouldn't
a pad and pencil be the first thing you would ask for? Why, they
are standard equipment at even directors' meetings.

In some courts, it is true, jurors are allowed to take notes. I think
this is true in England. There is a picture hanging in the office of
the Clerk of the United States Circuit Court in Boston which shows
one juror taking notes, with the juror behind him trying to read
them, one beside him yawning. They are allowed to take notes in
Georgia, unless they take so many as to distract their attention. And,
as we know, the jurors who tried the Knave of Hearts for stealing
the tarts were provided with slates, on which they all wrote very
busily. Bill the Lizard, indeed, used a pencil that squeaked. This

was more than Alice could stand and she took it away from him, but he went on writing with his finger, and it left no mark. But by and large jurors are not encouraged, and even forbidden, to take notes of the testimony they are supposed to be listening to.[22] I will take the law of Indiana, because it leads to an interesting colloquy on the subject. The Supreme Court of Indiana ruled, "The juror is to register the evidence as it is given, on the tablets of his memory and not otherwise." [23]

The colloquy I refer to took place in the Indiana State Bar Association not very long ago, in 1948. The question was whether jurors should be allowed to take notes.[24] Mr. Bomberger argued that they should be allowed to. "It seems inconsistent to permit a trial judge, trained in the art of hearing and weighing evidence, sitting with or without a jury, to take notes of the evidence, and to deny to jurors, with little or no experience, the right of this aid to their memory during their deliberations. . . It is well-known that, especially in lengthy trials, jurors get into a state of helpless confusion and contradiction as to important facts." [25]

I suggest that the law quite deliberately means to throw the jury into as much helpless confusion as it decently can. For the law has only two choices, and one is impracticable. The law could either ask the jury to make a thorough and complete study and analysis of all the evidence, such as a lawyer does to prepare his argument on appeal. This is impracticable. Or the law could ask the jury to just listen. Any middle ground would be worse than either. For one thing is sure, the evidence has to be taken as a whole, not only all of it, but as a whole, all at one look. So anything short of a thorough restudy of it would be not simply confusing, but misleading. And yet I suspect a deeper reason. Mr. McNagny, who argued against Mr. Bomberger that the jury should not be allowed to take notes, put this reason in two short sentences. "Many of our people are unduly impressed with the importance of the written word. This is one prejudice which we need not carry into the jury room." [26] You cannot put it better.

Another thing is the requirement of unanimity. It is a corollary of the expectation that the jury's verdict will be a total assertion. Miss Emmet goes on to say, after the paragraph I have quoted, "When we make a positive total judgment with our whole being, we say that we have faith in the object concerning which it is made. 'Total,' therefore, can also be taken as referring to the fact that the judgment is an act of the whole man. I have said, following Professor Stocks, that it is an assertion about the character of the object as a whole. But we may of course be mistaken in thinking that we have grasped the character of the object as a whole. Nevertheless, the attempt to do this, and not merely to give assent to those of its aspects which can be analyzed in terms of discursive reason (or 'partial assertions'), calls for an integrated response of the whole man, and therefore the term 'total assertion' can be taken to refer both to the intended object of this judgment and to the way in which the judgment is made. Such judgments can be distinguished, as we have seen, from beliefs based on estimates of probabilities, and also from judgments of the self-evidence of logical arguments which could, of course, also be described as examples of assent given freely and at the same time seem to be necessitated. The latter judgments consist in intellectual assent to arguments the steps of which are clearly articulated. The total assertion is not an argument, but an act of evaluation, and so includes emotional response." [27]

Unanimity assumes a solidarity which, as we have seen, is discouraged by the law. The answer to this, I think, is that we want the jury to act only on our common conscience, on what is almost immediately obvious, not on what is elaborated by a little group. It is also curiously alien to a people whose other institutions are built round the rule of a majority. Speaking of the Navahos, Kluckhohn and Leighton say, "The native way of deciding an issue is to discuss it until there is unanimity of opinion or until the opposition feels it no longer worthwhile to urge its point of view." "The present practice of actually voting for candidates or on policy decisions is a white innovation and still makes most older and middle-aged Navahos uncomfortable." [28]

Finally, the law refuses to let the jury give any reasons for its decision. Lord Goddard, the Lord Chief Justice who presided in Harold Laski's libel suit against the newspapers in 1945, put it this way when he charged the jury. "Another incalculable advantage of trial by jury is this: whereas, if a judge tries a case, he has to give the full reasons on which he bases his judgment, a jury are in a more fortunate position, that they cannot be cross examined or asked to give their reasons; they simply return their verdict one way or another, say what they find and they do not give their reasons." [29]

Of course a jury should not be asked to give its reasons, for one thing because it can't. Even judges find it difficult to give the reasons which brought them to their decisions. As Holmes said, "Judges know how to decide a good deal sooner than they know why," [30] and "Lawyers, like other men, frequently see well enough how they ought to decide on a given state of facts without being very clear as to the *ratio decidendi*." [31] We want the judges to explain themselves for two very good reasons. We want their minds as well as their courtrooms to be open to the public. And a man who knows that he is expected to give reasons for what he does is the more likely to act logically and rationally. But the jury is interpreting and administering a part of the law which would be denatured by explanation. The jury is applying patterns of behavior of which they are scarcely themselves aware. To recur to Pascal, the jury is proceeding, as we want them to proceed, on principles which are too numerous and too subtle for expression. No one can express them, and only a few are even aware of them. If the jury or the jurors were expected to give reasons for their verdict, not only would they not be the reasons on which they in fact acted, but the knowing that reasons were expected of them would change the very nature of the judgment we want the jury to give.

For in some matters we are not satisfied with judicial decisions which ignore the subliterate patterns of behavior and the subtleties which the law itself, alone, and by its very nature, is incompetent to interpret to us. Professor Harold J. Berman says, "There is a law in the minds of men, a wholly unofficial law—what the pre-revolutionary Russian jurist Petrazhitsky called an 'intuitive law.' . . . Not only does each person have his own conceptions of rights, duties, privileges, powers, and immunities—his own law-consciousness—but there is also a group law-consciousness— a 'socially adapted intuitive law'—which evolves in the various communities to which we belong; family, school, church, factory, commercial enterprise, trade or profession, neighborhood, city, region, nation—each has its own rules of conduct, its own unofficial and largely unwritten pattern of obligations and sanctions. The positive law proclaimed by the state cannot do violence to the law-consciousness of the people without creating serious tensions in society." [32]

Only Pascal's *esprit de finesse* can apply this "socially adapted intuitive law" to the occasions on which we want it evoked. This is the jury's function, and I think it can be inferred from the fact that the law cherishes and nurtures a creature so alien to its own ideals, so hostile to its boast that this is a government of laws and not of men, and so subversive of its usual complacency that the law is the embodiment of reason. How else can you explain the presence of this changeling?

The law calls in a jury not only when it lacks confidence in its judges, but when the law lacks confidence in itself. There was once a people, more civilized than we are yet, who had such confidence in themselves that they dispensed with judges. The Athenian courts in the fifth century were composed only of a jury, no judge at all. What's more, the Athenians were not satisfied with the short sampling of only a dozen. They made their juries as precisely reflective of the Attic people as they could, by juries of a hundred, five hundred, fifteen hundred, who were drawn by an intricate system of lot from all their communities.[33] The more important the case, the more the Athenians multiplied the peculiar characteristics of a jury by increasing the number of jurors. Socrates was tried by a jury of 501. When Alcibiades was tried for treason, it was by a jury of 1501. They were a people who had confidence in themselves.

Either we lack such confidence in ourselves or we are too busy with other things to sample ourselves by more than a dozen of us. So we hedge our bet on ourselves by selecting our juries. Take our blue-ribbon juries in New York. They were held constitutional by the Supreme Court in *Fay* v. *New York* [34] in the spring of 1947. But it was only five to four, over the protests of Murphy, Black, Douglas, and Rutledge. They said there is "a constitutional right to a jury drawn from a group which represents a cross-section of the community. And a cross-section of the community includes persons with varying degrees of training and intelligence and with varying economic and social positions. Under our Constitution, the jury is not to be made the representative of the most intelligent, the most wealthy, or the most successful, nor of the least intelligent, the least wealthy, or the least successful. It is a democratic institution, representative of all qualified classes of people. . . To the extent that a 'blue ribbon' panel fails to reflect the democratic principle, it is constitutionally defective." [35]

Murphy, Black, Douglas, and Rutledge were the better Athenians, but the majority were better constitutional lawyers. There is nothing in the Constitution which prevents us from putting the more rational of us on our juries, nor from judging this quality by the rule of thumb of social or even financial success. And yet are we so sure that the more rational a citizen is the better he fulfills the irrational and intuitive element in our law, without which a court would be incomplete, only part of a man, sitting in judgment upon whole men?

In the course of a discussion following a lecture which Professor Jerome Michael gave to the Association of the Bar of the City of New York in the spring of 1950, he said, "At this point I am going to say something which you may find very shocking. Judge Coleman is supposed to submit an issue to the jury if, as the judges say, the jury can decide reasonably either way. But to say that I can decide an issue of fact reasonably either way is to say, I submit, that I cannot, by the exercise of reason, decide the question. That means that the issue we typically submit to juries is an issue which the jury cannot decide by the exercise of its reason. The decision of an issue of fact in cases of closely balanced probabilities, therefore, must, in the nature of things, be an emotional rather than a rational act. . ." [36] Is it so certain that the more rational of us have the finer and the more reliable emotions? A jury can be as tenderly perspicacious as it can be ruthless.

Let me wrap up pretty much all of what I have been trying to say about the jury in the words of Mrs. Louise Koch. She stepped down out of the jury box after the acquittal of one Herbert Gehr for second-degree murder. In Carmel, New York, in January 1951, Gehr had shot and killed his wife through the screen door of his cabin in the woods, where his wife and three detectives had caught him, just before dawn, with another woman. Gehr told the jury that he thought his wife and her escort of detectives were prowlers, and insisted that he had killed his wife by accident. On the first ballot the jury stood nine to three for second-degree manslaughter. "Then we discussed it," Mrs. Koch said, "and decided that we would have done the same thing if we had been in Mr. Gehr's place." *

I'll stand on Mrs. Koch's remark. This is precisely the function of the jury as I see it, and in fact the way I think a good jury works. As the jury is a microcosm of society, so too the trial court, judge and jury, is a microcosm of the individual. In the judge we have our intellectual side. In the jury, we have the intuitive part of us. Together they reflect each of us as the jury reflects all of us. And a society which does not trust itself may be a state, but it is not a society at all.

Ethics in the Law

I have referred to our common conscience and to patterns of behavior without even apologizing for not making it clear what I meant. I have plainly implied that in the operations of the trial court, and specially in the functions of the jury, there was something which is in the law and yet not of the law, something which is part of the law and yet distinguishable from it. I have implied this without ever giving it a name. It is time I explained myself.

I am going to call it ethics, though "ethics" is an unruly and sometimes disobedient dog, with a way of running off ahead of you to the reader and not coming back when you call him. There are other words. When Holmes was explaining why he believed in leaving cases of negligence to a jury, one reason, he said, was that it introduced "popular prejudice" into the administration of the

---

* *New York Herald Tribune* and *New York Times*, January 17, 1951; and if the judge had told them that this was the proper basis for their verdict it would have been error. So, at any rate, it was in the case of *Louisville & Nashville Ry. Co.* v. *Gower*, 85 Tenn. 465 at 474, 3. S.W. 824, 827 (1887), where it was held error for the judge to instruct the jury that due care was "Just such care *as one of you*, similarly employed, would have exercised under such circumstances." For, said the court on appeal, "It does not appear that all or any of the members of the jury were men of ordinary prudence." Yet this is just what they were supposed to be. What else is ordinary prudence than how prudent ordinary men would be? And what better sampling of ordinary men than a jury?

law.[37] He was only sharpening his point. I'd rather try to discipline the dog Ethics, but before I do let me emphasize one thing. I am not setting ethics off against law. What I am referring to is in the law. It is a component of law just as the oil as well as the vinegar is a component of a salad dressing. To slip into the language of logic, what I am calling ethics is not a contrary of what you may be thinking of as law, but a subcontrary. The presence of one does not exclude the other. The more there is of one, the less there is of the other, and both are present in the application of any generality to any particular occasion.

Now let me try to make myself clear. The whole of law may be divided into four quadrants, and what I am calling ethics is one of them. I will begin by describing briefly the other three quadrants.

In one quadrant—I will call it the northwest—extends that area of our activities in which the law leaves us free of any legal liabilities and obligations. Here ethics may owe allegiance to religion, but not to the law. The only function of the law is to respect and protect our ethical freedom. Most systems of law, whether in Rome or in England, are as much concerned with indicating the area within which men are free to act as they choose as they are concerned with delimiting the area within which men are required to act or not to act in a specific way. Of these the former is much the larger and more important. Max Radin said, "Not only what we ought to do or not to do, but what we may do if we choose or leave undone if we prefer, is the business of the law." [38]

Take birth control and the distribution of contraceptives as an example. Here ethics is happily free to entertain, indeed it welcomes, quite contrary views. There is a moral judgment which holds birth control by the judicious use of contraceptives to be a positive good, and another which holds it to be a positive evil, a sin. The law takes no part in this conflict of ethical duties. It not only stands neutral, willing to accept with equal good will whichever side it is politically compelled to take, neither requiring us to use contraceptives nor forbidding us to buy them (except in Massachusetts and Connecticut). Until then the law protects our freedom to do as we choose, to be damned if we do or blamed if we don't.

The law does well to keep out. It only does harm when it is compelled to enter. It only cheapens the ethics it touches. For the law, I think by its very nature, has a lower standard of satisfaction than ethics. The law calls for only a minimum standard. You may go as near to breaking the law as you care or dare to do without breaking it, as Holmes pointed out. "The fact that it [the company] desired to evade the law, as it is called, is immaterial, because the very meaning of a line in the law is that you intentionally may go as close to it as you can, if you do not pass it." * If you don't, the law is satisfied. There is no such thing as a twinge of law, as there is a twinge of conscience. Ethics, on the other hand, has a very different kind of standard, indeed two standards, a maximum as well as a minimum, like some thermometers. What Hugh Whitney said about God is true of ethics. God, he told me, is easy to please, but impossible to satisfy.

In the opposite quadrant, to the southeast, let us say, lies what the law calls *mala* merely *prohibita*. Here we may be legally bound, but we are ethically free, for our activities which the law here either prescribes or forbids are of a kind in which ethics takes no interest. The rule of the road is the stock example. It is a matter of ethical indifference whether we are told to keep to the right or to the left. Much of conveyancing, the law of future interests, the rule against perpetuities, all the ritual of the law, as in the execution of a will or a deed or in the consideration required of a legally enforcible contract, and the like lie in this quadrant. This is the arid part of the law, where "reason is the life of the law, nay the common law itself is nothing else but reason," as Coke said.[39] Here the law can be logical, for here it is capable of very nearly precise statement.

In neither of these quadrants are ethics and law anything but neighborly. In the other two, northeast and southwest, they become intimate. In one, call it northeast, they are antagonistic, for here lies the duty of civil disobedience. It is here that we are sometimes confronted with an obligation, which is surely ethical, because it

---

* *Superior Oil Co.* v. *Mississippi,* 280 U.S. 390, 395–396 (1930). And the case of the pawnbroker doing business without a license. "It may be assumed that he intended not to break the law but only to get as near to the line as he could, which he had a right to do, but if the conduct described crossed the line, the fact that he desired to keep within it will not help him. It means only that he misconceived the law." *Horning* v. *District of Columbia,* 254 U.S. 135.

can't be anything else, to break the law; witness Thoreau, and his Duty of Civil Disobedience. I'll come back to Thoreau.

It is of the remaining quadrant that I want to speak, where ethics and law coöperate to the same end, and when we obey one we obey the other at the same time. Our problem is to decide what part ethics plays in the law. The part that the law plays in ethics is simple, easy, and obvious. The law simply offers its aid to enforce what ethics only bids us do. What the law does for ethics is procedural. What ethics does for the law, and in the law, is substantive, and since they are both addressed to the same purpose it is hard to tell them apart.

I suggest that ethics has two, and perhaps only two, peculiar enough characteristics to make it possible to tell ethics from law when they are working together to the same end. I don't know how much what I have to say will help moralists and philosophers. Probably not very much. I do hope, however, that it will comfort those who are unsettled by the mistaken belief that ethics and law are always contraries which are to be contrasted, instead of being, here in this quadrant, merely distinguishable, colleagues as well as competitors.

Each of these two characteristics may best be described in terms of its source. For one of these sources we may start with moral codes. Whitehead says, "Moral codes have suffered from the exaggerated claims made for them. The dogmatic fallacy has here done its worst. Each such code had been put out by a God on a mountain top, or by a Saint in a cave, or by a divine Despot on a throne, or, at the lowest, by ancestors with a wisdom beyond later question." [40]

What Whitehead meant by the dogmatic fallacy he had already explained. "The error consists in the persuasion that we are capable of producing notions which are adequately defined in respect to the complexity of relationship required for their illustration in the real world. . . Except perhaps for the simpler notions of arithmetic, even our more familiar ideas, seemingly obvious, are infected with this incurable vagueness. . . Our task is to understand how in fact the human mind can successfully set to work for the gradual definition of its habitual ideas. It is a step by step process, achieving no triumphs of finality." [41] We are not, therefore, to confound a code with its interpreters. Though interpretation may purport to do no more than expound an ancient, even a dogmatic, code, yet it may at the same time be a new application of an old principle, and so be later wisdom. Specially is this likely to be the case when the interpreter pretends to an equal infallibility, for then further and later interpretations must, as well as may, be likewise infallible, and earlier pronouncements equally fallible. I am tempted, but I don't know enough about the doctrine of papal infallibility to use it as an example.

But a man may be his own interpreter. A man may very well believe that he is his own best interpreter to himself. He may even undertake to write his own text in terms of symbols of his own self-esteem, his intuitive personal preferences, his own Can't Helps, in Holmes's phrase. Ayer used to call moral judgments feelings of approval or disapproval.[42] Later he regarded this as an oversimplification. His elaboration comes under my second point.

This source of ethics, therefore, leaves us with nothing that comes to us from any higher source than ourselves, nothing more imposing than what some of us, or even each of us, think or feel about what the rest of us do, and which the rest of us are as free to reject as they are to offer. Not authority, but likemindedness or likeheartedness, by way of birth or by way of education, is the reason under this theory, and the only reason, for the similarity we see in the precepts and judgments of ethics. Ethics is, then, as individualistic as humanity can be and as the law is not.

This is my first distinction and criterion of ethics. For the law must try to be as equalitarian and uniform in its orders and applications as it dare, dealing with the average man, the median man, the man *moyen sensuel,* not, as ethics does, with each of us individually.

I offer two examples of a vein of ethics in the law which may be detected by this first touchstone. One is a question of business ethics. Under the Sherman Act the question has been raised whether a company which has reached a certain size in proportion to its market and which occupies more than a certain fraction of its chosen field has the same freedom in the conduct of its business and in its choice of business practices as a company of less proportionate size and position. May a large enterprise not do what a smaller enterprise may legitimately do? Does size, and consequent power, of itself restrict a company's freedom of action? May the same practice be an unreasonable restraint of trade by the one when it is not by the other? Does what is right become wrong simply because the doer is more powerful?

The question cannot be evaded by putting it in terms of fact instead of law. To be sure, a cuff over the ear from Joe Louis might be harder to take than a squared-off punch from less of a man, but to say that the act of Joe Louis is not really the same act as the corresponding act of the average man, simply transfers the difference from the act to the doer, and this offends one of the virtues of the law on which we most securely rely, that the law is no respecter of persons and that the law treats every man alike.

No. If we should answer the questions I have asked affirmatively, it would indicate to me that we have come upon an ethical doctrine in the law, the doctrine of *noblesse oblige*. We should be saying that solely by virtue of a man's excellence or the superiority of his talents, skills, and powers, he is held to a higher standard of obligation and liability. We should be depriving him of the right to regard himself as one of us and of conducting himself and his affairs like his fellows. Likewise with the qualities of mercy, pity, and compassion for our weaker brethren, which I suggest are equally ethical and equally unlegal.

Another example appears where the law makes a distinction between the liability of a person of reasonable prudence and intelligence and the liability of a person of superior intelligence. Here the *noblesse* of superior intelligence brings a man within the scope of an obligation when a strict equality of treatment would leave him outside. The Restatement of Torts says (italics mine):

"(1) The words 'reason to know' are used throughout the Restatement of this Subject to denote the fact that the actor has information from which a person of reasonable intelligence *or of the superior intelligence of the actor* would infer that the fact in question exists or that such person would govern his conduct upon the assumption that such fact exists.

"(2) The words 'should know' are used throughout the Restatement of this Subject to denote the fact that a person of reasonable prudence and intelligence *or of the superior intelligence of the actor*

would ascertain the fact in question in the performance of his duty
to another or would govern his conduct upon the assumption that
such fact exists." [43]

My second point of distinction rests on the concern which ethics
shows for the particular occasion. It is derived from another view
of the source of ethics, the one which sees the strength of ethics in
social esteem as well as, and even more than, in self-esteem. I suppose the truth is that these are two views of the same thing. Peirce,
I think, made this clear. "Conscience really belongs to the sub-
conscious man, to that part of the soul which is hardly distinct in
different individuals, a sort of community-consciousness, or public
spirit, not absolutely one and the same in different citizens, and
yet not by any means independent in them. Conscience has been
by experience, just as any knowledge is; but it is modified by
further experience only with secular slowness." [44] Was not Pascal
saying much the same thing? "The Stoics say, Reënter into yourselves. It is there that you will find your repose. And that is not
true. The others say, Go out of yourselves; seek your happiness in
diverting yourself. And that is not true. Disorders come. Happiness is neither outside us nor inside us. It is in God, and neither
inside nor outside of us." [45]

As I have said, Ayer came to believe that his early view that
"moral judgements are merely expressive of certain feelings, feelings of approval or disapproval" was "an over-simplification." Later
he said, "The fact is rather that what may be described as moral
attitudes consist in certain patterns of behaviour, and that the expression of a moral judgement is an element in the pattern. The
moral judgement expresses the attitude in that it contributes to
defining it." [46] Strip ethics of its religious vestments, down to the
bare and visible skin, and it is no more than conforming to the
patterns of your fellows, associates, neighbors, friends, intimates,
all those others of mankind whose opinions you regard with a decent respect.* We are out of the subjective into the objective; or,

* Perhaps this is an oversimplification in the other direction. Professor
Henry D. Aiken says that the moral judgment "appeals not to the private in-
clinations of the listener, but to the socialized dispositions which he possesses
as a member of society. The speaker pronounces the judgment, as it were, not
as an agent, but as a *carrier* of meanings whose effective appeal is determined

as the anthropologists put it, we are out of a guilt-culture into a shame-culture.[47]

Now mark one characteristic of these patterns. They are living things. They shift and change. They alter their complexion and their tone with secular slowness, but they are never still. They are not principles, which are uniform, even permanent. They are occasional. Every ethical judgment which is based upon these patterns has its time and place, its here and now, its there and then, and it is never quite valid anywhere else or at any other time.

Law boasts its constancy. Ethics may not be so wise, but it is shrewder. Ethics says to the Law, "You deal with the usual man in the usual situation. I admire you, but I don't see how you do it. I deal with this man in this situation. I admire your ability to ignore the singular, though seldom, injustices which you commit for the sake of your ideal—which, mind you, I do not share—of equality and order, but it strikes me as an odd sort of justice. It may be that you are right, but I won't admit that I am wrong."

We are at the confluence of two streams. The dark waters of the individual soul and the roiled waters of social esteem mingle as they flow down into the clear blue logic of the law. Or we are standing on the banks—metaphors are easily manipulated—and we watch the turbulent waters flow by. It makes no odds. There are two sorts or sides to what we call ethics. One of them makes a point of the particular individual, the other of the particular circumstance. Both converge on some unique occasion. The point is, this is something the law itself is incapable of doing.

Patterns of Your Behavior

This double distinction between ethics and law should help us to recognize ethics when we meet her, but they scarcely tell us much about the lady. The philosophers have had much to say, but they

---

elsewhere. And the listener is moved by it, not simply because it happens to coincide with some half-aroused private emotion which he happens already to feel, but because, as a socially conditioned organism, the rules of society are already written into his nervous system as conditioned patterns of response." Aiken goes on to elaborate and illuminate this in "The Authority of Moral Judgments," *Philosophy and Phenomenological Research*, vol. XII, No. 4 (June 1952).

have usually been talking to each other about properties and values.
Holmes threw up his hands and called it Can't Helps. He was right,
of course, but it's no help. He also told Pollock that ethics was
". . . a body of imperfect social generalizations expressed in terms
of emotion." [48] I don't know what Holmes meant by "imperfect,"
unless he meant not legally enforceable, like an imperfect obligation, but I think it is a mistake to confine ethics to the emotions,
even to the mild emotions of approval or disapproval. The fact is,
emotional language expresses only the speaker. It describes how he
feels, not what he is talking about, and the more emotionally he
speaks, the more he is expressing himself. A moral judgment rendered in emotional terms is either a boast or a confession.

Emotional language leads us into hopelessly inconclusive and
eventually futile questions, such as what is "moral turpitude." I do
not myself think that making moonshine whiskey involves moral
turpitude, and I cannot see how intelligent people can argue whether
it is or not, unless for fun. It comforts me that Black, Frankfurter,
and Jackson agreed that this phrase "has no sufficiently definite
meaning to be a constitutional standard for deportation." [49]

But then what shall the law do when it has to decide such a
question as whether a man has a "good moral character"? *Repouille*
v. *United States* [50] was a case of euthanasia. Repouille had chloro-
formed his young son, who was an idiot and a monstrosity, mute
and blind, who spent his life in a crib, and had to be fed. He had
four other children, all dependent on him for support. Judge Frank,
dissenting, said, "I incline to think that the correct statutory test (the
test Congress intended) is the attitude of our ethical leaders." But
the precedents persuaded him to be "guided by contemporary public opinion about which, cloistered as judges are, we have but vague
notions." He added, skeptically, "One recalls Gibbon's remark that
usually a person who talks of 'the opinion of the world at large,' is
really referring to 'the few people with whom I happened to converse.'"

Contemporary public opinion, even when it is picked up in casual
conversation, is surely a better source for what we are looking for
than the attitude of our ethical leaders. They are our leaders. We
don't want them to rule over us. But I think we've got to go deeper
than opinion. Let me elaborate on the patterns of behavior, which

Ayer referred to, for I think they are the stuff of which the ethics we are looking for is made.

If we agree, as I think we must, that one of the purposes of the law is to make each other's future behavior as predictable as we can, then those in authority—legislatures, policemen, government agents—play only a small part. It is what the corner grocer, the friendly barkeeper, your employer, parson, priest, parents, friends, wife, and children do and say that counts. It is what they expect of us that really steadies our behavior on predictable courses, much more than what the authorities prescribe for us. To be sure, we want to make the future better as well as predictable, and often their expectations will do this too, but prediction comes before manipulation. We must have some idea of how the men and women with whom we have to live will otherwise behave, before we undertake to make them behave better. The crowbar needs a fulcrum. The soil of society needs humus as well as fertilizer.[51]

When the anthropologists saw that they were running out of primitive cultures, they began to take an interest in their own. I take it that Robert and Helen Lynd were the first, with their *Middletown*, in 1928. The anthropologists then perceived something about the law which jurists, except for some gifted spirits like Karl Llewellyn, had ignored. The anthropologists perceived that the law was only the explicit and articulate part of what existed in all cultures and was still implicit in the primitive cultures they had been studying. Jurisprudence was an anthropology of the literate part of our culture. Jurists then began to understand that their law not only reposed upon a base of what Sumner had called folkways or mores, and what Ruth Benedict was calling patterns of culture, but contained these within itself. These folkways, these mores, these patterns were part of the law, and perhaps the most important part of it.

Ruth Benedict describes these patterns like this: "The life-history of the individual is first and foremost an accommodation to the patterns and standards traditionally handed down in his community. From the moment of his birth the customs into which he is born shape his experience and behaviour. By the time he can talk, he is the little creature of his culture, and by the time he is grown and able to take part in its activities, its habits are his habits, its beliefs his beliefs, its impossibilities his impossibilities. Every child that

is born into his group will share them with him, and no child born
into one on the opposite side of the globe can ever achieve the thou-
sandth part. There is no social problem it is more incumbent upon
us to understand than this of the rôle of custom. Until we are intelligent as to its laws and varieties, the main complicating facts of
human life must remain unintelligible." [52]

"Society," she says, "is only incidentally and in certain situations
regulative, and law is not equivalent to the social order. In the simpler homogeneous cultures collective habit or custom may quite
supersede the necessity for any development of formal legal authority. American Indians sometimes say: 'In the old days, there were
no fights about hunting grounds or fishing territories. There was no
law then, so everybody did what was right.' The phrasing makes it
clear that in their old life they did not think of themselves as sub-
mitting to a social control imposed upon them from without. Even
in our civilization the law is never more than a crude implement of
society, and one it is often enough necessary to check in its arrogant
career. It is never to be read off as if it were the equivalent of the
social order." [53]

The difficulty is, we are only scarcely aware even of the existence
of these patterns in our behavior. For, as Miss Benedict says farther
on, they are the very stuff of our own thinking, the lens without
which we cannot see. I suspect that what Selden had in mind was
not religion, but these patterns, when he said, "We look after religion as the butcher did after his knife, when he had it in his
mouth." [54] Whitehead remarks that "it requires a very unusual mind
to undertake the analysis of the obvious." [55] It takes a mind at least
a little out of the ordinary to appreciate even the existence of the
obvious, and these patterns are obvious because we are offered no
alternative course of conduct except to break them.

Clyde Kluckhohn says, "In our highly self-conscious Western civilization that has recently made a business of studying itself, the
number of assumptions that are literally implicit, in the sense of
never having been stated or discussed by anyone, may be negligible.
Yet only a trifling number of Americans could state even those implicit premises of our culture that have been brought to light by
anthropologists. If one could bring to the American scene a Bush-
man who had been socialized in his own culture and then trained

in anthropology, he would perceive all sorts of patterned regularities of which our anthropologists are completely unaware." [56]

We are unaware of these patterns because they are a part of us, and we take ourselves too much for granted to pay attention to what is a part of us. It calls for too much detachment. We can see them better in the past than in the present, better among others than among ourselves. Nevertheless they are there, in our statutes, judicial doctrines, administrative rules and regulations, contracts, leases, wills, and all the other legal documents which compose the law. Nothing a lawyer can write or a judge must read is even intelligible until we read into it the patterns of so much of a man's behavior or conduct as conforms to his understanding of what his fellows expect of him. His understanding is a matter for psychology, and so also the reasons why he conforms to others' expectations. So, too, I take it, their expectations are for the social psychologists. But the pattern of what we do, our behavior and conduct, to which a man conforms his own, is also the business of the law.

Lawyers long ago admitted a few of these patterns into the law under the credentials of custom and of morals, but they stopped short. Lawyers insisted that custom must be both immemorial and universal before it could be admitted. They were too conservative. As to morals, they were too restrictive. Why should lawyers recognize only those patterns of behavior which it is a sin for us to ignore? There is more to life than a quiet conscience. But not all lawyers. In *The Sense of Injustice*, Cahn says, "The free citizen legislates for himself by appreciating the intentional value of jural situations, as his private sense of injustice becomes more and more immanent in the public conscience. The sense of injustice that contributes to the making of law inheres in him; it has its being and its sanction in his endowment. Legal order becomes his order; the rewards of compliance and the penalties of infraction are less outside than within." [57]

I am spreading the meaning of ethics exceedingly thin, but not, I think, thinner than it must be spread in the law. For we are talking about ethics in the law and the part it plays there, and we have to cover a great deal, almost all, of the law. And need I remind you of what the distinguished lawyer said to my friend, who called on him when he was sick? "I've been trying to think of any occasion in a man's life when he would not be the better off for legal advice; and I can't." I hope you are nearer to admitting the truth of this than you were at first.

An Immanent Order and an Imposed Order

I have spread ethics so thin that we are brought to another distinction which reaches far beyond the distinction between ethics and law. We are brought to the distinction between the two great orders of which any law is composed, an immanent order and an imposed order.

When Ruth Benedict tells of the Indians' saying, "There was no law then, so everybody did what was right," she was referring to the immanent order in the law. When she called the law crude and arrogant, she was thinking only of the imposed order. But the law is neither so crude nor so arrogant as she supposed, for it includes both orders, as the distinguished lawyer knew.

These terms, an immanent law and an imposed law, are Whitehead's, and he had best explain them himself. All we need to do is apply specifically to the law what Whitehead is applying generally to the cosmos.

In *Adventures of Ideas,* Whitehead says, "By the doctrine of Law as immanent it is meant that the order of nature expresses the characters of the real things which jointly compose the existences to be found in nature. When we understand the essences of these things, we thereby know their mutual relations to each other. Thus, according as there are common elements in their various characters, there will necessarily be corresponding identities in their mutual relations. In other words, some partial identity of pattern in the various characters of natural things issues in some partial identity of pattern in the mutual relations of those things. These identities of pattern in the mutual relations are the Laws of Nature. Conversely, a Law is explanatory of some community in character pervading the things which constitute Nature. It is evident that the doctrine involves the negation of 'absolute being.' It presupposes the essential interdependence of things."

This doctrine, Whitehead goes on to say, carries consequences with it. "The exact conformation of nature to any law is not to be expected. If all the things concerned have the requisite common character, then the pattern of mutual relevance which expresses that character will be exactly illustrated. But in general we may expect that a large proportion of things do possess the requisite character and a minority do not possess it. In such a case, the mutual relations of these things will exhibit lapses when the law fails to obtain illustration."

Moreover, "since the laws of nature depend on the individual character of things constituting nature, as the things change, then correspondingly the laws will change. . . Thus the conception of the Universe as evolving subject to fixed, eternal laws regulating all behavior should be abandoned."

Whitehead contrasts an Imposed Order. "The doctrine of Imposed Law adopts the alternative metaphysical doctrine of External Relations between the Existences which are the ultimate constituents of nature. The character of each of these ultimate things is thus conceived as its own private qualification. Such an existent is understandable in complete disconnection from any other such existent: the ultimate truth is that it requires nothing but itself in order to exist. But in fact there is imposed on each such existent the necessity of entering into relationships with the other ultimate constituents of nature. These imposed behavior patterns are the Laws of Nature. But you cannot discover the natures of the relata by any study of the Laws of their relations. Nor, conversely, can you discover the laws by inspection of the natures." *

---

* Whitehead, *Adventures of Ideas,* pp. 142–144. Michael Polanyi made a similar distinction between what he called General Authority and Specific Authority, in his Riddell Lectures, given in 1946. Quine told me about them after I had used, and got used to, Whitehead's Immanent and Imposed Orders. Polanyi has the advantage of steering clear of essences. He is talking about science and scientists, but he uses the law as an example and he finds the same two orders running through religion. Michael Polanyi's *Science, Faith, and Society* (London: Oxford University Press, 1946). Unfortunately, they are out of print, so here are four pertinent paragraphs:

"The art of scientific work is so extensive and manifold that it can be passed on from one generation to the next only by a large number of specialists, each of whom fosters one particular branch of it. Therefore science can exist and continue to exist only because its premises can be embodied in a tradition which can be held in common by a community. This is true also of all complex creative activities which are carried on beyond the lifetime of individuals. We may think for example of the law and of the Prot-

You see how nicely these four paragraphs apply to our little legal
world. Rid "immanent" of any of the mystical, or religious, or theological meanings which you find in the dictionary, and then for
the things which compose nature substitute the individuals which
compose the community. The common elements in their various
characters raise patterns in their mutual relations. These patterns
are the immanent order in our law. As for the imposed order, un-

---

estant Christian religion. Their continued life is based on traditions of a
structure similar to that of science and it will help us to understand tradition in science—and also prepare us for the more general problems of society with which we want to deal later—if we proceed now to include such
fields as law and religion in our further discussion.

"We have seen how science is constantly revolutionized and perfected by
its pioneers, while remaining firmly rooted in its tradition. Each generation
of scientists applies, renews, and confirms scientific tradition in the light of
their particular inspiration. Similarly we see judges deriving from past judicial practice the principles of the law and applying these creatively in the
light of their conscience to ever new situations; and see how in doing so they
revise in many particulars the very practice from which they derived their
principles. Similarly to the Protestant the Bible serves as a creative tradition
to be upheld and reinterpreted in new situations in the light of his conscience. While the Bible is held by him to mediate to the individual the
revelation which it records, belief in this revelation is held to acquire the
full value of faith only when it is affirmed by the individual's conscience.
Conscience can then be used even to oppose the authority of the Bible where
the Bible is found spiritually weak. . .

"The realms of science, of law, and of Protestant religion which I have
taken as examples of modern cultural communities are each subject to control by their own body of opinion. Scientific opinion, legal theory, Protestant
theology are all formed by the concensus of independent individuals, rooted
in a common tradition. In law and in religion, it is true, there prevails a
measure of official doctrinal compulsion from a centre, which is almost entirely absent from science. The difference is marked; yet in spite of such
compulsion as legal and religious life are subjected to, the conscience of the
judge and of the minister bears an important responsibility in acting as its
own interpreter of the law or of the Christian faith. Thus the life of science,
the law, and the Protestant Church all three stand in contrast to the constitution, say, of the Catholic Church which denies to the believer's conscience
the right to interpret the Christian dogma and reserves the final decision in
such matters to his confessor. There is here the profound difference between
two types of authority; one laying down general presuppositions, the other
imposing *conclusions.* We may call the first a General, the latter a Specific
Authority. . .

less we accept "a God on a mountain top" or "a Saint in a cave," I don't know where we shall find an imposed order except in our law.

Whitehead says that in the immanent order "the exact conformation of nature to any law is not to be expected." Only if every one concerned has the requisite common character will a pattern be exactly illustrated. For the minority who do not possess it, the law lapses.

"The main contrast between a régime of General Authority such as prevails in science, the law, etc., and the rule of a Specific Authority as constituted by the Catholic Church lies in the fact that the former leaves the decisions for interpreting traditional rules in the hands of numerous independent individuals while the latter centralizes such decisions at headquarters. A General Authority relies for the initiative in the gradual transformation of tradition on the intuitive impulses of the individual adherents of the community and it relies on their consciences to control their intuitions. The General Authority itself is but a more or less organized expression of the general opinion—scientific, legal, or religious—formed by the merging and interplay of all these individual contributions. Such a régime assumes that individual members are capable of making genuine contact with the reality underlying the existing tradition and of adding new and authentic interpretations to it. Innovation in this case is done at numerous growing points dispersed through the community, each of which may take the lead over the whole at any particular moment. A Specific Authority on the other hand makes all important reinterpretations and innovations by pronouncements from the centre. This centre alone is thought to have authentic contacts with the fundamental sources from which the existing tradition springs and can be renewed. Specific Authority demands therefore not only devotion to the tenets of a tradition but subordination of everyone's ultimate judgement to discretionary decision by an official centre.

"We see emerging here two entirely different conceptions of authority, one demanding freedom where the other demands obedience."

I may add a few sentences. Polanyi's General Authority imposes our premises upon us. "The premisses of freedom will thus be secured by compulsion, exercised by public opinion either directly or through the process of legislation." (p. 58) And, "We must have sovereignty atomized among individuals who are severally rooted in a common ground of transcendent obligations." (p. 58) Polanyi has avoided essences, but not the antinomies in freedom and in compulsion. "Freedom of this kind, it would seem, must be described in the particular as freedom to act according to particular obligations. Just as a person cannot be obliged in general, so also he cannot be free in general, but only in respect to definite grounds of conscience" (p. 51). Who has been able to avoid this antinomy? Has Whitehead? I like to think so.

This puts a different face on disobedience. Knaves can and do break the law, as do fools, sots, and clowns, for, as Emerson said, they make the fringes of the tapestry of life.[58] The pattern does not run into the fringes. For such folk there is nothing but an imposed order. But it is quite otherwise with the recalcitrants, the protestants, and the non-conformers. The Tolstois, the Gandhis, and the Thoreaus, who recognize a duty of civil disobedience, are conforming to a pattern of their own. For them our immanent law simply lapses in favor of another immanent law. "If a man does not keep pace with his companions," Thoreau said, "perhaps it is because he hears a different drummer."

Thoreau refused to pay his poll tax. He chose instead to spend the night in the Concord jail, and there he said this to himself. "The proper place to-day, the only place which Massachusetts has provided for her freer and less desponding spirits, is in her prisons, to be put out and locked out of the State by her own act, as they have already put themselves out by their principles. . . I saw that, if there was a wall of stone between me and my townsmen, there was a still more difficult one to climb or break through before they could get to be as free as I was. I did not for a moment feel confined, and the walls seemed a great waste of stone and mortar. I felt as if I alone of all my townsmen had paid my tax." [59]

The recognition of an immanent order in our law allows us to deal with the vexing problem of the reconciliation of liberty and duty. Under an imposed order, our liberties must rely on our rights against the state. Our Bill of Rights is the Charter of our Liberties. Civil obedience is the negation of liberty. The noble statement, In Thy Service is Perfect Freedom, remains a paradox. Lord Acton, on the other hand, insisted on identifying liberty with morality. "Liberty and morality. How we try to separate them—to found liberty on rights, on enjoyments, not on duties. Insist on their identity. Liberty is that condition which makes it easy for conscience to govern. Liberty is the government of Conscience—Reign of Conscience." [60] This is true, but only in an immanent order of law, for there conscience does govern, and the reign of law is indeed the reign of conscience.

I grant you I may not be taking conscience in as religious or as theological a sense as Acton did, but the Reign of Conscience need not be the Kingdom of God. "Conscience really belongs to the sub-conscious man, to that part of the soul which is hardly distinct in different individuals, a sort of community-consciousness, or public spirit, not absolutely one and the same in different citizens, and yet not by any means independent in them." [61] I am taking conscience to be not the cause, but the vehicle of ethical conduct, as Leslie A. White put it. Let me try to state White's explanation of the nature of what we call our conscience. It is not, I quickly say, what Hamlet said made cowards of us all. On the contrary, quite on the contrary for Hamlet meant introspection and inward doubt, White means, and I mean, what saves us from solitude and fright, our kinship with our fellows.

Conscience is not any inborn physiological ability to tell right from wrong, as our ears give us a sense of balance and tell us when we start to sway out of the vertical. Conscience, White tells us, is the sense which makes us aware of cultural and social forces, as the canals in our ears make us aware of the forces of gravity. Or, for another analogy, White says that "the human organism lives and moves within an ethical magnetic field, so to speak." Whatever the analogy, by our consciences, he declares, "society not only succeeds in enlisting individuals in the cause of general welfare, but actually causes them to work against their own interests—even to the point of sacrificing their own lives for others or for the general welfare." What's more, "the individual is made to feel that it is *he* who is making the decision and taking the proper action, and, moreover, that he is perfectly 'free' in making his decision and in choosing courses of action."

Let me interrupt to say that we all admire things that we do not wholly understand simply because they are larger than we are, but I did not appreciate how astute as well as powerful they were, these cultural and social forces which guide our lives and at the same time are able to persuade us that we are independent of them.

White concludes, and proves his thesis, as follows, "That conscience is a cultural variable rather than a psychosomatic constant is made apparent of course by a consideration of the great variation of definition of *rights* and *wrongs* among the various cultures of the world. What is right in one culture may be wrong in another. This follows from the fact that an act that will promote the general welfare in one set of circumstances may injure it in another. Thus we find great variety of ethical definition and conduct in the face of a common and uniform human organism, and must conclude therefore that the determination of right and wrong is social and cultural rather than individual and psychological. But the interpretation of *conscience*, rather than custom and mores, in terms of social and cultural forces serves to demonstrate once more that the individual is what his culture makes him. He is the utensil; the culture supplies the contents. Conscience is the instrument, the vehicle, of ethical conduct, not the cause. It is well, here as elsewhere, to distinguish cart from horse." [62]

These Orders in Your Law

I suggest that what Whitehead says about the Laws of Nature fits our laws. The only difference that I can see is this. Whitehead offers the two orders as alternative doctrines. The Laws of Nature are either immanent or they are imposed. It depends on which view of them you take, which theory of the cosmos you adopt. In our legal world, the immanent and the imposed are not mutually incompatible alternatives. They coexist and maintain themselves and each other in the same law. They share our law. The more there is of one, the less there is of the other, until in the extreme the lack of one brings chaos, and lack of the other anarchy.

There is, I believe, a correlation between the amount of immanence in a law, that is, the extent to which it relies upon our patterns of behavior, and the degree of generality and vagueness in its terms. The outward and visible sign of immanence in a law is the degree of generality with which it is expressed. For not only is it true that the more general the terms in which a law is couched and the vaguer they are, the greater the delegation of power and discretion to the courts to give them meaning. It is also true that general terms and vague terms rely upon our acceptance and compliance. A law which is imposed upon us is a command, and a command, if it is to be effective, must be particular. It may be made particular by the definite terms in which it is itself expressed, or made so by the enforcing agency in rules and regulations, or even by arbitrary action, but in one way or another the cutting edge of a law of the imposed order must be sharp. The medium through which the immanent order expresses itself is, on the other hand, the vague word, which falls to the floor like an empty sack without an immanent content. It's a gunny sack, not a box or a carton.

Take any of them—negligence, defamation, fraud. Has any of these words more meaning than the immanent ordering of our common lives gives it? Take cruelty as a cause for divorce. It is no more than a compendium of the ways we do not expect a man to treat his wife, or a wife her husband. Defamation is no more than what we do not expect a man to say of his neighbor, or even of anyone else who might bring suit. And so of all the vague terms in which the great bulk of the law is expressed, through to the words which take all their meaning from their context, like reasonable, fair and equitable, detrimental to the public interest, and due process of law. On the other hand, where the law expresses itself more precisely, there we may be sure that the law is imposing commands upon us, and not just stiffening the patterns which we have delineated for ourselves and woven into our lives.

Of course a law which undertakes to impose its commands upon us should be precisely stated, as precisely as possible, for its strength, as well as its justice, lies in its predictability. Else how can we be expected to conform our conduct to its prescriptions? Lawyers may be justly proud of their prowess in precise statement, for they are the technicians of the imposed order, but they need not be ashamed of their talent in the much more difficult art of writing as vaguely and imprecisely as the patterns in our behavior are themselves vague and imprecise. For here the strength of the law lies in its adherence to the pattern. Here the law is not a command, but a statement. It is law in the scientific sense, a law of our nature, if not of all Nature. If you state a pattern more precisely than in fact it is, you do something to it. You leave something out of it, much as a photograph leaves out what a painting tries to put in. Something happens to all human relations when you try to put them accurately and precisely into words. It is not only that you cannot do it, but you do something to those relations, unless you use words of the precisely correct degree of vagueness, and so leave us to fill your words out with our meanings from the patterns in our lives. When President Lowell established the Harvard Houses, he used to say that he was going to make as few regulations as possible, rather he wanted to give the Houses their own traditions as soon as possible.

This is the wisdom of the law. The more the law can rely on our patterns, the less it need impose itself upon us, and the better off it is. But there is a further wisdom. The ethics we have found in the law is little more than a descriptive ethics, descriptive of nothing much better than our common behavior. It is not the ethics of our best behavior. It is an ethics which is no more normative of our life than a dictionary is of our language. For the function of the law is not to make us virtuous, but to leave us free to be. The law can no more make us excel in virtue than a thesaurus can make us into authors or a rhyming dictionary into poets. The business of the law, as Max Radin said, is not only to tell us what we ought to do or not to do, but to keep open the area in which we are free to act as we choose. It would be intolerable if this were not so. For then we should need another Saint Augustine to remind us that there is nothing praiseworthy in doing what we ought to do, or another Saint Paul to insist that "if righteousness come by the law, then Christ is dead in vain." [63]

Courts of Appeal

A Progression of Judgments

There is a progression of judgments beginning with that which nearly every witness, almost unavoidably yet sometimes as deliberately as he dares and the lawyers will let him, passes on the events he is describing. The lawyers pass judgment—a biased judgment, as in duty bound—on the witnesses' testimony. Then the trial court passes its judgment. Finally the court of appeal passes the final judgment on the trial court's judgment on the witnesses' judgment. Each, in the exercise of its function, judges the exercise of the function of the instrument of justice next nearer to the conduct which started the judicial process. Each criticizes the other in the only way one can criticize another's work, from a larger perspective, which puts the particular event against a larger background, and therefore in more general terms.

But in this progession there is a significant and important break between the trial court and the court of appeal. Courts of appeal are at a great disadvantage, and they are intensely aware of it. Trial judges are startled by the difference when they are promoted to a court of appeal or called in to sit on appeal. Not only must they learn to think in a new perspective, they find that personalities have become only names and that events have been washed and sterilized in the printed word. This is why the rules of procedure insist that "the findings of fact" of the trial court must stand unless "clearly erroneous." [1] This rule rests on these handicaps on a court of appeal, so far removed from the particular case and so reliant on the printed word. As Learned Hand said, "It is idle to try to define the meaning of the phrase, 'clearly erroneous'; all that can be profitably said is that an appellate court, though it will hesitate less to reverse the finding of a judge than that of an administrative tribunal or of a jury, will nevertheless reverse it most reluctantly and only when well persuaded." And in cases where the trial judge's findings depend upon whether witnesses spoke the truth, "the accepted rule is that they 'must be treated as unassailable.' The reason for this is obvious and has been repeated over and over again; in such cases the appeal must be decided upon an incomplete record, for the printed word is only a part, and often by no means the most important part, of the sense impressions which we use to make up our minds." [2]

Courts of appeal have a way of comforting themselves with what I may call the culinary theory of appeal and review. This is to regard an appeal simply as a review of the way the case was tried by the trial court, its method, its manners, its procedure, its technical handling of the case. It is the way of a cook who has such faith in his recipe that he cannot believe that the pudding will not be palatable if the recipe has been followed, such faith that he wouldn't taste it even if he could, such faith that it can't be good if the recipe was not followed. Now it is nearly always true that a conscientious cook with a good recipe does make good bread, and we should be fools to underestimate the importance of procedure in the law. There can be no justice without legal procedure, and we must not think too ill of lawyers who believe that this is all there is to justice. But it is not necessarily true. Remember the Sacco-Vanzetti case. The trial judge, Judge Thayer, had shamed himself, but off the bench, not in court. On the bench, in court, he had followed the rules. If injustice was done, I'm inclined to think the fault lay with the jury, who were suffering under the prevalent hysteria of the time, which is the price we pay for making the jury so like ourselves. But the Supreme Judicial Court of Massachusetts made no attempt to find out whether justice had been done. It did no more than the statutes then required it to do, which was simply to see if the rules had been followed; and they had been followed, no more and no less. The Court did not even sniff, far less taste, the dish.

Plainly the culinary theory is not good enough, for all its virtues. Look at the way we changed the meaning of "due process of law."

This phrase once meant no more than it says, proper judicial behavior: proper notice of the charges against you and a hearing, where you have the right to confront and cross-examine the witnesses against you, to produce and examine your own, to testify yourself if you chose, but with the privilege of not incriminating yourself. These are the essentials, which is sufficiently proved by the way we take them for granted until we are deprived of them and have to fight for them again. However, this procedural meaning was not good enough. In the demanding decades that followed the Civil War, we were able to persuade the Supreme Court of the United States that the phrase really reflected the bright face of Justice herself. The upshot of judgment as well as the approach to it had to be considered, the product, as well as the process, the what as well as the how. The Court was led to consider what, in effect, the trial court had done, and not simply and severely, how it had gone about doing it. It is significant, and I think it illuminates my point, that the Court started this expansion, and popularization, of the phrase, due process of law, in reviewing the activities of tribunals other than courts. It began with state commissions setting railroad rates, which not only lacked the dignity of courts but were far from expert in judicially due process.[3]

Justice exists only in the particular case. Only there can justice be done, and this is what the trial courts are trying to do. So too are the courts of appeal, in spite of their handicaps, but they have another function, which is the direct and inevitable consequence of these very handicaps. Courts of appeal are also providing justice for the next case. The very fact that courts of appeal have only the written word to work with gives their judgments a permanence which the judgments of the trial courts, working with oral and visual material, cannot possess; and the fact that courts of appeal work at a farther remove from the actual and the concrete, and therefore have to express their opinions in general terms, make their judgments inevitably applicable to similar future cases.

This is the peculiar and important function of courts of appeal, and this is the one I want to examine. They are explaining, and so giving meaning to the words in which the law is expressed, and not simply applying their extensive meaning to particular occasions. They are giving the words their intensive meaning, if you recall the distinction, their full meaning, which the trial courts apply extensively.

I shall try to demonstrate this by the way the Supreme Court gives meaning to the Constitution, for its exalted position and the magnitude of its work makes it the best example. Possibly too good. We have demanded more of our Supreme Court than we have any right to ask of any court of appeal, even the highest.

Your Ambulatory Constitution

I like to think that We the People of the United States, in whose name the Constitution was drafted, as you can see in the preamble, did in fact execute it and that we are constantly adding our names to those of the Convention of 1787. This may be fanciful, but it is none the worse for that. It is a metaphor, and, as MacLeish says, "A world ends when its metaphor has died." [4]

At any rate, in lawyer's language, the Constitution is an ambulatory document that continues to speak in the present, rather than the day and year it was dated. We are speaking—not the Constitutional Convention, not the First Congress adopting the Bill of Rights, not the Thirty-Ninth in the Fourteenth Amendment—and We are still speaking. We are speaking as I write, and We'll be speaking when you read.

It is equally important, it seems to me, to consider to whom We are speaking. The Constitution is not really a single document, except typographically. Different parts of it are addressed to different persons. Thus, the Third Article, which is on the judiciary, is addressed to the Supreme Court itself, telling the Court its jurisdiction, etc. It is speaking to Congress in the important section eight of the First Article where Congress' legislative powers are set down; and also in section nine, which prohibits Congress to pass bills of attainder, export duties, and other things. The Bill of Rights, that is, the first ten amendments, is addressed to the Federal Government, though the First Amendment reads as if it were speaking only to the Congress. The Fourteenth Amendment is addressed to the States. Throughout the document we find that different parts are addressed to different persons, and each in his own situation and on his own occasion may interpret the words very differently. Even the same word may mean different things when it is addressed to different people; since it is the person addressed who will first give a meaning to the word or phrase on a particular occasion.

To be sure, the Supreme Court will have its own opinion of what the constitutional words mean and, when they are addressed to the Court, this will be the meaning, for there is no one else to correct the Court. But when they are addressed to someone else, the Court uses its meaning only as an alternative, to help it judge the propriety and the reasonableness of the meaning which some other agency of our government has already given to the words.

It was no accident that, barring the egregious Dred Scott case, up to 1868 all the Acts of Congress which the Supreme Court held unconstitutional related to the courts.[5] The Constitution was speaking directly to the Court. When Chief Justice Marshall established the doctrine of judicial supremacy and the power of the Court to hold an Act of Congress unconstitutional, in *Marbury* v. *Madison* in 1803, it was under the Third Article of the Constitution relating to the jurisdiction of the Court. Marshall was interpreting words which were addressed directly to his Court. The Court had a better right to interpret them than Congress had.

In the Dred Scott case, in 1857, in a fit of political arrogance, the Court undertook to say that a Negro whom the State of Illinois had freed and made a citizen could not be a United States citizen. This was not the Court's particular business. The Constitution was speaking to the states and to Congress, not to the Court. The decision was an egregious failure, rejected by President Lincoln in his First Inaugural, overwhelmed by the Civil War, and ignored.

It is harder to understand why the difference between giving meaning to words which are addressed to yourself and giving meaning to words which are addressed to others was not perceived by the Court when it really began to exercise judicial supremacy after the Civil War. To be sure, the Court professed great respect for the opinion of Congress and the state governments, but paying the respect due to dignity and prestige is not the same thing at all as recognizing a difference in function. Passing only a secondary and critical judgment on the meaning which the person directly addressed and immediately concerned has already given to the Constitution, instead of at once giving it your own meaning, is more than a matter of courtesy or even deference. Your respect for another man's position, or for his competence, or for his wisdom has a bearing upon your judgment as to whether his opinion was right or reasonable. The more you respect him, the better prepared you are to accept his opinion. But this is not the same thing as recognizing that your judgment is no more than a judgment on his judgment.

The functional difference also goes deeper than perceiving the difference in degree of definition and precision between language addressed to the courts and language addressed to legislatures and administrative agencies. The one is likely to be legal and technical. The other is almost sure to be the large language of laymen. Frankfurter and Reed drew our attention to this difference in degree of precision in their dissent in the Tidewater Transfer case which I have already quoted.[6] As they pointed out, the subject matter of Article III of the Constitution on the judiciary was technical, unlike the "great concepts like 'Commerce . . . among the several States,' 'due process of law,' 'liberty,' 'property' [which] were purposely left to gather meaning from experience."

These large vague general phrases, like commerce, due process of law, liberty, property, do not "gather meaning from experience" of themselves, just because they are large and vague and untechnical, no more than a vacuum fills itself. Too many of the Justices, and too often a majority of the Court, have insisted that these and other such large phrases had already been amply and adequately filled with the wisdom of our ancestors to allow us to think that either their size or their generality was alone a sufficient reason why they have been "expanding with experience." Too many chapters in the history of the Court must be devoted to bitter battles over whether these words should be allowed to expand, to make their expansion with experience simply the result of their generality. What made them expand, what sometimes distended them, was the influence into them of our experience, and our experience flows into them because their meaning is first determined, not by the Court but by the other agencies of our government which are in immediate charge of its operation. It would be intolerable if our Court were to draw solely upon the wisdom of the Founders for the meaning of our Constitution. We cannot have our government run through the middle of the twentieth century as if it were stuck in the end of the eighteenth.

"What's past is prologue, what to come in yours and my discharge," [7]
as the Duke of Milan said.

No more can the meanings of the words in our Constitution, under
which our agents are running the country, be other than our own
present current meanings of those words. For the Court cannot
fairly judge the reasonableness or propriety of the meanings which
they, the other agencies of our government, have given these words
on any other standard or theory than that by which they interpreted
them. This may come hard to some lawyers, but I see no escape
from the fact that the Court must speak the same language as that
in which the rest of the business of our government is conducted.

Meaning for Essence

It would be a hazardous enterprise to attempt to state, as now
seems necessary, a general theory of meaning, but I don't propose
to go any farther than I need, and no farther than I dare.

In an earlier chapter, I drew on the logicians for the theory of
what they call the extensive meaning of words, but this, as I have
said, flattens the meaning of a word down to two dimensions. Courts
of appeal, especially the Supreme Court when it is interpreting the
Constitution, are not only applying words to particular occasions.
They are giving meaning to words for use on future occasions. They
need a theory of three dimensional meaning. The extension of a
word answers only the question, What does this word refer to? or,
What is this word true of? This calls for no more than a theory of
reference, as I hope I have made clear. What we need now is a
theory of meaning, which will help us to understand how we give
meaning to words. A theory of reference tells us how to aim our
piece and how to score hits and misses. Anyone who makes a career
of firearms wants to know more about them than that.

I will start with Aristotle. We almost always do start with him
anyway, whether we know it or not, because we have been brought
up on him. He is the author of our underlying tacit assumptions, and
we take them for granted, as part of our common understanding,
or misunderstanding, of things. We are dyed with his metaphysics.
I start with Aristotle because some of his metaphysics colors the
paragraphs which I quoted from Whitehead on an immanent order,

and unless the dye is washed out, it will lead to a misunderstanding of the relation between the meaning of words and the immanent component of law. I will approach Aristotle in the company of a modern logician. Quine says,

"The Aristotelian notion of essence was the forerunner, no doubt, of the modern notion of intension or meaning. For Aristotle it was essential in men to be rational, accidental to be two-legged. But there is an important difference between this attitude and the doctrine of meaning. From the latter point of view it may indeed be conceded (if only for the sake of argument) that rationality is involved in the meaning of the word 'man' while two-leggedness is not; but two-leggedness may at the same time be viewed as involved in the meaning of 'biped' while rationality is not. Thus from the point of view of the doctrine of meaning it makes no sense to say of the actual individual, who is at once a man and a biped, that his rationality is essential and his two-leggedness accidental or vice versa. Things had essences, for Aristotle, but only linguistic forms have meanings. Meaning is what essence becomes when it is divorced from the object of reference and wedded to the word." [8]

This is what we must do, divorce the Aristotelian essence from the thing we are talking about, the particular piece of behavior or the course of conduct which is claimed to be unconstitutional, and marry essence to the words, which then becomes their meaning.* The essence of a thing consists in those of its qualities or properties without which it would cease to be itself. That's metaphysics, and "muddle-headed" anyway, Bertrand Russell says.[9] The meaning of a word, on the other hand, consists in those properties which the word connotes, that is, those properties which, when we apply the word to anything, we imply that the thing possesses. That's linguistics. By and large, except by accident, we see little more than

---

* C. K. Ogden and I. A. Richards, *The Meaning of Meaning* (2nd ed.; New York, 1927), pp. 187, 188, say that essences, "by those who do not let their realism overpower their criticism may best be regarded as Connotation hypostatized." And connotation "is a selection of properties or adjectives; but properties are not to be found by themselves anywhere, they are fictitious or nominal entities which we are led to feign through the influence of the bad analogy by which we treat certain parts of our symbols as though they were self-complete symbols. We have no justification, beyond this bad analogy, for treating adjectives as though they were nouns."

what we look for. We find what we seek, and when we don't know what we seek, we don't usually find anything. Meanings have as much right to primacy as things. Where would be the beauties of nature without art? The artist shows us what to look for. Then we see it.

The transformation from metaphysics to linguistics is none the less radical for being easy to perform. Simply put the word in quotation marks. There is a good example in the opinions in *Eisner* v. *Macomber*, where the Court held that a stock dividend was not income under the Sixteenth Amendment. The opinion of the majority speaks of "the characteristic and distinguishing attribute of income . . . considering its essential character. . . Having regard to the very truth of the matter. . ." All quite Aristotelian. Holmes, with Day, dissenting, says, "I think that the word 'income' in the Sixteenth Amendment should be read in a sense. . ."[10] Holmes and Day were talking about a word. The majority were talking about a thing.

Now if you will look back at the paragraphs I quoted from Whitehead, you will see that he speaks of the essences in things, "the characters of real things," and "the essences of these things." I am denying, or at any rate disbelieving, that things have essences. I don't know that they haven't. But the point is, it does not matter. Divorce essence from things and wed it to the word, and it becomes meaning, and we have our immanent order of law where it belongs, in the meanings of words. And as for the imposed order, where will you find an actually imposed order except in the law, unless we go to a god on a mountain top or to a saint in a cave? Law is the despot on a throne. Legislation is a genuine act of imposition. I suggest that Whitehead's distinction between the two orders is peculiarly applicable to the kind of law with which we are concerned. Whether or not it is valid anywhere else, is none of our business.[11]

Quine used the stock example of the rationality of "man" and the two-leggedness of "biped." Let us take some examples from the law.

Does the admiralty jurisdiction of the Federal Courts extend to a particular body of water? In the early days of the Republic, the Supreme Court refused to take jurisdiction in admiralty over any but tidal waters. Unless the particular body of water on which the cause of action arose had the essential property of ebbing and flooding with the tide, the Court left the case to the state courts. Thus in 1825, in the case of a vessel called the "Thomas Jefferson," Story, speaking for the Court and following the English law, held that its admiralty jurisdiction was confined to tidal waters. In England all the navigable waters were tidal. The English law had picked on tidal as the essential property, and Story was Aristotelian enough to be convinced that the Court could not enlarge its admiralty jurisdiction to include non-tidal inland waters, however navigable, unless, of course, they had become tidal through the process of nature. It was a matter of physical fact.[12] In a case twenty odd years later, in 1848, the Court split over the question of fact whether the Mississippi was tidal as far up as the place where the collision takes place.[13]

Story was thinking in terms of the essential property of certain bodies of water. But in 1851, in the case of Genessee Chief, under Taney, the Court changed the meaning of the phrase to include navigable waters. In Aristotelian terms the Court extended its jurisdiction to cover two kinds of waters, navigable as well as tidal, but the Court was quite aware that what it was doing was changing the meaning. "It is evident," the Court said, "that a definition that would at this day limit public rivers in this country to tide-water rivers, is utterly inadmissible." Moreover, the Court made it clear that this change in meaning reflected, not any change in the properties of the country's inland waters, but a change of policy. It referred to the earlier case as "an erroneous decision into which the court fell, when the great importance of the question as it now presents itself could not be foreseen. . . For the decision was made in 1825, when the commerce on the rivers of the west and on the lakes was in its infancy, and of little importance, and but little regarded compared with that of the present day."[14]

Take a "bill of attainder" which Congress is forbidden to pass by Article 1, Section 9, of the Constitution. What is it? What does the phrase mean?

It is quite clear what an attainder used to be and what the word used to mean in England and the colonies. As Frankfurter said in the Lovett case in 1946, "The distinguishing characteristic of a bill of attainder is the substitution of legislative determination of guilt and legislative imposition of punishment for judicial finding and sentence. . . All bills of attainder specify the offense for which the attainted person was deemed guilty and for which the punishment was imposed. There was always a declaration of guilt." But the Court decided that the essence of a bill of attainder was not this, but "the infliction of punishment without a judicial trial." [15]

You see there are two points of view, the Aristotelian and Quine's. From the Aristotelian point of view, it makes no sense to say about any particular body of water that the ebb and flow of the tide is essential to admiralty jurisdiction, and that navigability is not; or vice versa. Nor does it make any sense to say about a particular Act of Congress which deprives some individual of the opportunity to work for the Government, which was what Congress did to Lovett, that a declaration of guilt is essential and the imposition of a punishment is not; or vice versa.

Are we not better able to understand what the Court is doing if we take the point of view that it is changing the meaning of these words than if we insist that they are merely describing or reflecting the essential properties in the things to which the Court is asked to apply them? Indeed how do we know that these things have any properties peculiar to themselves? After all we are dealing with their significance to us, not with their significance to anyone else, and least of all with their significance to themselves, if that makes any sense.

It seems to me that the Aristotelian notion of essences is plausible only when it is obvious. Thus it may be taken to explain why the Court applies a statute to a new situation or to new conduct which obviously possesses the appropriate essence, such as applying the word "commerce" to the telegraph and the telephone; and it explains those fortunately few occasions when the Court has to confess that it simply made a plain mistake, as for example, the Court's decision in 1944 to include the business of insurance in "commerce." [16] The Court had to retract what it had said in 1869 and in 1895, and reverse a decision it had made in 1913, all to the effect that "the business of insurance is not commerce." [17] All but one of the Justices agreed that insurance was commerce. The one was Jackson, who disagreed only because he thought that Congress, not the Court, should correct the obvious error.

The Supreme Court has dimly, but dimly, appreciated the difference between the two theories. In *Smith* v. *Allwright*, after a word on "the desirability of continuity of decision in constitutional questions," and after saying that, "when convinced of former error, this Court has never felt constrained to follow precedent," the Court said, "This is particularly true when the decision believed to be erroneous is the application of a constitutional principle rather than an interpretation of the Constitution to extract the principle itself." [18]

I take it that the extraction of a constitutional principle is the discovery and determination of the required essence and that the principle itself and its application is a meaning. The Court at least senses a difference, and feels more free to change a mistaken meaning than to announce the discovery of a different essence.

The practical objection to ascribing essences to things instead of meanings to words is not that it's metaphysics, muddled or not. The objection is that we are thereby led to think that the properties which make up the essence of a thing change only as the thing itself changes. The marriage of essence to things is indissoluble except by death or adultery. If things did have essences, I suppose this would be true. The advantage of a divorce and the remarriage of the essence to words, by which it becomes their meaning, is that it puts the properties within our reach and under our control, as, of course, the properties of things are not. As soon as we recognize that the essences which Aristotle taught us belong to things are really the meanings of our own words, we see that interpretation is a handicraft and not a speculation. This makes interpretation all the more difficult.

The trick is to pick out the properties which the word connotes. For some words this is pretty easy. The properties which we imply by calling a number even or odd, or by saying that there was a quorum present, can be singled out and distinguished from other properties as easily as picking coals out of a snowdrift. In the vocabulary of human affairs, on the other hand, connotations are not so neat a matter of black and white. But lawyers and judges need not be appalled or even impressed. It is their usual and familiar vocation to deal with words which are at once the most familiar and the most complicated and vexatious, those which concern the conduct of their fellow human beings. The art of the relevant and a sense for the important are the peculiar virtues of lawyers and judges. The Court is well fitted to find the meaning of the Constitution where it belongs, in its words. It may be easier, but I won't agree that it is nobler, and

I know it is not wiser, to chase the meaning of our Constitution through the back door of our ancestors' intentions. The Justices are at their best when they measure the opinions of their fellows and co-workers in our government against the meaning of the words, instead of against a reverence for the past.

And what is this meaning? If I am right in following Quine and washing the notion of essence out of Whitehead's immanent order of law, the meaning which the Court is seeking is the explicit and articulate part of the immanent component of our law, as much of it as can be expressed in words. So the meaning of the Constitution, and so too, in varying degree, the meaning of all the general terms in the law, is to be found in its immanent order.

The Supreme Court and Meaning

I want now to show how insistent We are, the People of the United States, that this should be so, that the Supreme Court should draw the meaning of the Constitution from our immanent meanings. My metaphor that We were constantly signing and executing that document was true, all but literally true. We are speaking, and the Court is our spokesman. The true story of our courts of appeal, and in particular the story of our Supreme Court, rises in a steep curve in response to our demands.

There is much to be said against the Court yielding to this demand, and it ought to be said, all the more because you may call it the crabbed view of a strict lawyer. It is not. It springs from the idealism of a radical democrat, as you will see.

The legal idea of the Constitution, and of the Bill of Rights particularly, is reflected in the restraints which the Supreme Court has laid upon itself when it is asked to pass upon the constitutional validity of legislation. I should leave out lawyers when they are advocates, for then it becomes their duty to ignore their political responsibilities. It is, then, not surprising that their clients are scarcely aware of these rules of self restraint. They were collected and restated by a quartet of judges of distinction, Brandeis, Stone, Roberts, and Cardozo. What they said, with Brandeis speaking for them, is classic and definitive.[19]

The Court is not to pass on the validity of legislation in a friendly proceeding. It must be a real law case. Nor should the Court anticipate a constitutional question. Only an immediate dilemma calls for a decision. Nor should the Court lay down a broader doctrine than the dilemma calls for. A constitutional question must be raised in the record. No one may attack a statute unless he is going to be hurt by it. No one may attack it and at the same time accept its benefits. And, finally, the Court should sooner construe a statute than strike it down. Briefly, the Court should not hold a statute unconstitutional unless this is the best way out of an unpleasant legal dilemma.

Some of these are simply rules of judicial procedure, to the end that a case which turns upon an interpretation of the Constitution may nevertheless be treated as a law case. Others are sound rules for the interpretation of any document, recognizing the respect due to the interpretation of the Congress or a State when the Constitution is addressed to them. But they are all in effect rules of abstention as well as self-restraint, and it is their reflection of the legal attitude toward the Constitution, and specially the Bill of Rights, with which we are now concerned. For the more the Court abstains, so it follows that only the worst statutes are unconstitutional, and to call a statute constitutional is no more of a compliment than it is to say that it is not intolerable. It makes constitutionality as low a standard of legislative and political morals as we could have, and yet have any at all.

That laymen are almost wholly unaware that the Supreme Court could have such a low standard of morals is as much the Court's own fault as anybody's. For the Court has too often relaxed its self-restraint on occasions which have excited publicity. No wonder, then, that we make the mistake of confusing our civil liberties with our constitutional rights. The Bill of Rights, freedom of speech and press, religious liberty, rights of assembly and petition, our rights against unreasonable searches and seizures, against self-incrimination, the right not to be deprived of life, liberty, or property without due process of law, and all the others, all these become the least of the liberties we want to enjoy. It is a bad habit, and a mean way of thinking, to hold up the Bill of Rights as our ideal of freedom. The Bill of Rights tells us only what we can go to law for, not what we can vote for. Our civil liberties are poorly served by being lumped with the least we have a legal right to insist on.

I heard the phrase I wanted on the radio not long ago, and I can think of few persons I should less like to borrow from or owe anything to than the speaker. It was Gerald B. Winrod who was speaking and finding fault with those who "took the Constitution for granted, like good health." That is just what I mean. We ought to take it for granted, just as we ought to take good health for granted. Constitutionality, so far as our legal rights are concerned, is no more than reasonably good political health.

It is strange that a people who are so proud of being democratic should turn for their liberties to the least democratic of their institutions. We turn to the Supreme Court, where the justices are appointed for life, whose salaries cannot be cut, who are removable only by the great process of impeachment, who are responsible really only to the traditions of the court. Why do we turn to them with more confidence than we do to the Congress, which we choose every other year? Charles Fairman, in the brightest, briefest, and best of the casebooks on constitutional law puts it this way: "To think of freedom of speech and of the press as some eighteenth-century heirloom, enshrined in the Constitution and guarded for us by the Supreme Court so that we have nothing to do about it but to enjoy it, is bad history and mischievous thinking." [20] And Judge J. Waties Waring said about the exclusion of Negroes from a primary election, "It is a shame and a disgrace for a case of this kind to come to a court. We do not need a judge to tell us if we are Americans." [21] Are we not able to be ourselves without being told how to?

We may well look to the courts for our constitutional rights, but we ought to get our own liberties ourselves and not expect the courts to give them to us. Some of you may listen to the Aldrich Family. On Thanksgiving night, in 1948, Charlie Clark suggested that anyone who didn't subscribe to the class picnic ought to be put on detention. Henry said this was against the Bill of Rights. "Where do you find anything about detention in the Bill of Rights?" asked Charlie. "It's there all right. Read between the lines, read between the lines."

When we feel the political morals of our legislatures, our Congress or our state legislatures, fall below our own, we turn to the courts for leadership into something better. However badly our representatives behave, however they caper, we never make the mistake of taking what they do or what they say as any indication that our standards or our ideals have fallen as low as theirs. Rather are we stirred. But instead of turning the rascals out, we turn to the Court. It is not to our credit, and yet we do it. The worse our representatives behave, the more we want to be told how much better they ought to behave.

This is the demand we make upon the Supreme Court, and it is no wonder that the Justices respond. No wonder the less faith we have in Congress or the state legislatures the less respect the Court owes to them, and the more the Court responds to our advances and our demands. No wonder that the Court tries to meet our expectations, tries to live up to them, tries to satisfy us. High expectations always bring out a man's best efforts. At the same time such flattery may go to his head. It certainly puts the Court into a very difficult and delicate position. How far should the Court go when we transfer more than a fair share of our available faith from Congress and the state legislatures to the Court and ask it to reject their interpretation of the Constitution? Two of the Justices, Murphy and Rutledge, in a burst of enthusiasm, once went so far as to announce that the Constitution, as they read it, "embodies the highest political ideals of which man is capable." [22]

I am not blaming them. They are answering our call for a braver world. They are victims of our confidence in them and our lack of confidence in ourselves. There is nothing more seductive than what people expect of you. Nor am I blaming, of course, the litigants who appeal to the courts to redress their own particular grievances—on the wildest, leanest hope of success that counsel will consent to argue. By all means let them wring the Bill of Rights. I am pointing the finger at all the rest of us who are content to lie back on the courts for what we ought to get up and do ourselves. What I find fault with is a complacent practice of expecting the judicial process to do the work and take the place of the democratic process. Our liberties are a company; free and eager, and angry, speech is their captain.

Who shall say the Justices are not justified? Not we who encourage them to do it. The fact is, the Court is acting under a head of demand of which we are scarcely aware, until the Court speaks. As the force of the wind may be judged by the belly in the sail, let us now try to appraise the demand we make upon the Court to pour our current political morals into our Constitution.

The best way is to illustrate it, first by some statements of individual Justices, then by two decisions of the Court.

Take the secret ballot. It did not come into our political life until 1888, when it was adopted by Massachusetts, and it came to us from Australia. You will find it in the Australian Constitutional Act of 1856. I need not say that it was unknown to our forefathers or that you will not find it in our Constitution. And yet Frankfurter, in the spring of 1950, said, "I do not suppose it is even arguable that Congress could ask for a disclosure of how union officers cast their ballots at the last presidential election even though the secret ballot is a relatively recent institution." [23] To be sure, he was not speaking for the Court. He was speaking his own thoughts on the oath required of union officers by the Taft-Hartley Act.

Illinois has given greater representation to its rural downstate counties than to its cities. A country vote meant more than a city vote. If you took the individual voter as the unit, some were given more political power than others. On October 21, 1948, just before the national election, the Court refused to hold this Illinois electoral law unconstitutional. Why, the Court said, our Federal Constitution itself "protects the interests of the smaller against the greater by giving in the Senate entirely unequal representation to population." [24]

But Douglas, Black, and Murphy dissented, and here is the way they undertook to get around the fact that the very Constitution on which they relied allowed the very thing to which they objected. "The fact that the Constitution itself sanctions inequalities in some phases of our political system does not justify us in allowing a state to create additional ones. *The theme of the Constitution* is equality among citizens in the exercise of their political rights. The *notion* that one group can be granted greater voting strength than another is hostile to *our standards* for popular representative government." [25]

These are my italics. Are not these three Justices substituting a new "theme" and new "standards" for the constitutional "notion" that the interests of a small group may be protected against a greater by giving it, as in the Senate, greater voting strength? The State of Illinois is composed of counties just as the nation is composed of states. I don't say it would not be an improvement, whatever havoc it would do to the United States Senate. All the same, it would take an amendment to make "equality among citizens in the exercise of their political rights" the theme of the Constitution.

Now I offer you two decisions of the Court. In the first the Court took a phrase which used to be as legal and technical as would please any lawyer and blew it up out of all legal recognition to meet an obvious moral necessity. The phrase is "a bill of attainder." The other decision involves a phrase which had, and still has, a perfectly plain and commonly understood meaning, and filled it up with experience, our experience. This is the phrase, "an establishment of religion."

A Bill of Attainder

In 1943 we were being hagridden by Congressman Dies, as we were later by Congressman Thomas and more recently by Senator McCarthy. Dies made a speech in the House demanding that the government be purged of "irresponsible, unrepresentative, crackpot, radical bureaucrats," and he named thirty-nine government employees. He urged Congress to refuse to appropriate money for their salaries.

The matter was referred to the Appropriations Committee, and a subcommittee held hearings, in secret executive session. It reported against three of the thirty-nine—Robert Morse Lovett, Goodwin B. Watson and William E. Dodd, Jr. You can find the kind of man Lovett was, and is, in *Who's Who*, or you can read his autobiography, *All Our Years*.

The House took thought and tacked a rider on an Urgent Deficiency Appropriation Act, that no money from this or any other act should be used to pay salaries to these three, except for jury duty or for service in the armed forces. The Senate Appropriation Committee promptly cut this provision out, and the Senate itself then voted unanimously against a conference report that left it in. The House insisted. The Senate yielded. And the President too had to yield. When Roosevelt signed the bill, he said, "The Senate yielded, as I have been forced to yield, to avoid delaying our conduct of the war.

"But I cannot so yield without placing on record my view that

this provision is not only unwise and discriminatory but unconstitutional." [26]

Watson and Dodd continued to serve without salary for a week
or so. Secretary Ickes persuaded Lovett to stay on, but after three
months, not to endanger future appropriations, he asked Lovett to
resign.

The three brought suit in the Court of Claims for their salaries
for the time they had worked and for which they had not been
paid. The Court of Claims found that the rider, section 304, was
"notable for what it did not do, as well as for what it did do. It did
not terminate the plaintiffs' services." [27] No, its sponsors knew very
well what they wanted and what they were doing; and they had
gone about it carefully and deliberately. So they did no more than
they thought necessary. Anyone, including the Supreme Court, who
wanted to block them, would have to go a long way to do it. [28]

The three appealed to the Supreme Court, and Black wrote the
opinion. He called the rider a bill of attainder. What is involved
here, he said, is a Congressional proscription of Lovett, Watson, and
Dodd, prohibiting their ever holding a government job. This rider
"clearly accomplishes the punishment of named individuals without
a judicial trial."

"Those who wrote our Constitution well knew the danger inherent in special legislative acts which take away the life, liberty, or
property of particular named persons, because the legislature thinks
them guilty of conduct which deserves punishment. They intended
to safeguard the people of this country from punishment without
trial by duly constituted courts. . . And even the courts to which
this important function was entrusted were commanded to stay
their hands until and unless certain tested safeguards were observed." These safeguards, Black said, include a jury, the right to be
represented by counsel, the right to be confronted by your witnesses, and so forth. And so too, he said, they proscribed bills of
attainder, and section 304 is just that. "Much as we regret to declare that an Act of Congress violates the Constitution, we have no
alternative here." [29]

Frankfurter's and Reed's dissent shows how far the Court had
gone. They agreed that the three should be paid for the services
they had rendered, but not that the rider was unconstitutional.

"Nothing would be easier than personal condemnation" of the rider,
they said, but "Not to exercise by indirection authority which the
Constitution denied to this Court calls for the severest intellectual
detachment and the most alert self-restraint." This is no bill of
attainder, they said, not, anyhow, as it was understood by those
who wrote the Constitution. "Their meaning was so settled by history that definition was superfluous. Judicial enforcement of the
Constitution must respect these historic limits." [30]

The Court had certainly gone a long way when it called section 304 a bill of attainder. Having made up its mind to kill this
thing for good, by a blow from the Constitution, all it could find
was the prohibition against bills of attainder. It was an antiquated
weapon, dull and rusty. But who will say that this rider was not
the modern equivalent of a bill of attainder?

We shall miss a point if we only applaud, and ignore the risk the
Court was taking, quite deliberately taking. What if Lovett had
refused to resign? What if Congress had then tacked another rider
to the next Urgency Deficiency Appropriation? It is not at all inconceivable. The Supreme Court had taken a chance. It had reached
and saved Congress from itself—always a hazardous thing to do,
saving anybody from himself. It had saved us from saving ourselves.

Suppose Congress had not only done the same thing again with
another such "bill of attainder," but also at the same time were to
take away the Court's jurisdiction to hear the next victim's appeal?
Then what? The Constitution gave Congress the power to do just
that. The Supreme Court has "appellate jurisdiction, both as to law
and fact, *with such exceptions and under such regulations as the
Congress shall make.*" [31] The Court had already once acknowledged
that Congress had this power, even when a case was pending before
it. When the Republican Congress in 1868 saw that the Supreme
Court was about to hold the Reconstruction Acts unconstitutional,
it prevented a decision by taking away the Court's jurisdiction.[32]
No, the Court's power is no more secure than it is divine.

The Court was taking a chance. And so were we. The House of
Representatives had made its intention very clear, to purge the government service of "irresponsible, unrepresentative, crackpot, radical
bureaucrats." If section 304 were constitutional, the way would be

open to cut off the pay of any government employee who offended irresponsible, unrepresentative, crackpot, radical Congressmen— from Cabinet members down to the women who work on their knees in the great paved corridors. Only the judges would be immune. Our forefathers had a considerate eye on judges. Whatever Congress could do to the Court, the Justices individually are pretty well protected. The only way of getting rid of them is by impeaching them, for their compensation "shall not be diminished during their continuance in office." [33] But not the Court. Its appellate jurisdiction could be taken away from it under the express language of the Constitution, much more clearly than Lovett's salary could be taken from him.

We appeal to the Court and the Justices listen. It comes hard not to, and their response is more admirable than our demand. It would be an easy conscience that failed to condemn what those Congressmen were doing in the Lovett matter. It was lack of conscience that allowed them to do it. A democracy that is willing to throw the burden of its decencies on its judiciary needs a conscience.

I do not know that any set of rules ever has been, or ever can be, worked out for the successful operation of a conscience.* It was easy enough for the Court to work out its simple cautionary rules of self-restraint and abstinence for the judicial review of legislation. If that function is grave and delicate, this new function is majestic. For it is nothing less than the political review of the Constitution itself in the light of a modern world, just as a statute is judicially reviewed in the light of the Constitution.

Such a prodigious and perilous task calls for action, not abstinence. It calls for a response, not restraint. If the Court is to be successful, it must act, and act boldly. But I do not suppose there is any need of teaching the Court to be bold. Pride is a judicial as well as an angelic sin, and arrogance is the occupational disease of judges. The old rules are still useful, lest the Court be too bold.

* Frankfurter's precepts are intellectual humility and rational standards. In *Dennis* v. *United States*, 341 U.S. 494 at 552, he said, "Our duty to abstain from confounding policy with constitutionality demands perceptive humility as well as self-restraint in not declaring unconstitutional what in a judge's private judgment is unwise and even dangerous." See also the last paragraph of his concurring opinion in *A.F. of L.* v. *American Sash and Door Co.*, 335 U.S. 538, 556–557, 1949.

And yet if the Court is to be free to act boldly, we must have some assurance that it will also act warily and thereby wisely. The best way to keep the Court wary is to keep the exercise of this prodigious power dangerous. By all means, therefore, let Congress retain an ultimate control over the Court's appellate jurisdiction. Let the judges sharpen their political wits on the whetstone of political peril. For what we are talking about is the most delicately difficult and dangerous of all government problems, that is, how power can be shared by two equal agencies when there are no words, no phrase, no formula by which we can divide the power between them. The Constitution makes no attempt to say which shall be the master on a showdown. Wisely, because there is no way of saying it. Congress and the President have all the force, if they dare to use it. The Court has nothing but its power to persuade us.

So, I say, let the Court live dangerously, that it may act wisely. The best way to see to it that the Court will guess right is to make it risky to guess wrong. What the Court must now work out for itself are rules of prudence as well as rules of self-restraint.

We too often forget that the reason for the great power of the Supreme Court is not that it interprets the Constitution to us, but that it reads our immanent patterns of behavior into our Constitution, and as it reads them into it, the Court explains them to us, and so makes us the more aware of them. And if it stresses the patterns of our better behavior, this is no more than the normative element in any good description. When enough of us kick against the pricks, the Court must save its face as best it can. But when enough of us do agree, or will agree, then the power of the Court is so tremendous that we find it hard to believe that such power is not imposed upon us, that it is only evoked from us, that the Court is only making explicit to us what was already implicit in us, and that it is we who are moving the mountain.

An Establishment of Religion

My other example is the released time programs in our public schools, time out of school hours for religious instruction by priest, pastor, or rabbi, whomever the pupil's parents choose. The First Amendment says that "Congress shall make no law respecting an establishment of religion, or prohibiting the free exercise thereof."

It is manifest that released time for religious instruction does not prohibit the free exercise of religion. On the contrary, it encourages its exercise and leaves it to the free choice of the parents. If released time runs counter to the Amendment, it must be in some sort "an establishment of religion." Now this is rather a precise phrase, "an establishment of religion." Madison, who drafted and proposed the Bill of Rights and who saw it through the First Congress, is as good a mundane source for what it meant as there is. Madison said that "he apprehended the meaning of the words to be, that Congress should not establish a religion, and enforce the legal obserjvation of it by law, nor compel men to worship God in any manjner contrary to their conscience." [34]

Look there upon that picture, and on this of what the Court has been saying; and let me at the same time say that I thoroughly agree with the Court. In *McCollum* v. *Board of Education* the Court held unconstitutional one of the several versions of the released time program in our public schools. In this case it was time out of school hours for religious instruction by your own or your parents' choice of priest, pastor, or rabbi on the school premises.[35]

It was an exceedingly difficult decision to make, although only one Justice, Reed, dissented, and it will sharpen the point I want to make if I first say why it was so difficult. The Court was asked to separate church and state just where the two are all but inextricable, in the education of the young. Louisa Clark put it briefly and neatly in her review of Professor O'Neill's book on *Religion and Education under the Constitution*. "Assuming that it is now unconstitutional for a state to give impartial as well as discriminatory subsidies to religion, is it likewise unconstitutional to aid religion-in-education? Any distinction seems in theory implausible, but in practice it touches the heart of the difficulty. For it is one thing to declare the mutual independence of the civil and religious spheres when thinking in terms of Locke's limited and neutral state. It is quite another to exejcute the principle in the disputed area of education. To do so Americans have had to divide education into two parts—the secular, entrusted to the state; and the religious, taught by church and home." [36]

Now let's see how the Justices handled it, and compare what the Court said with what Madison "apprehended the meaning of the words to be." I need quote only two sentences near the end of Black's opinion for the Court,

"For the First Amendment rests upon the premise that both religion and government can best work to achieve their lofty aims if each is left free from the other within its respective sphere. Or, as we said in the *Everson* case, the First Amendment has erected a wall between Church and State which must be kept high and impregnable."

You see the Court was relying, not on the words of the First Amendment, but on its "premise," what "can best work to achieve" its aims; or, alternatively, not on the First Amendment at all, but on a metaphor, for the "wall" is nothing more. A good metaphor, one of Jefferson's best, and I do not decry metaphors, but it is not the language of the First Amendment.

Frankfurter, Jackson, Rutledge, and Burton concurred. They said, "We are all agreed that the First and the Fourteenth Amendments have a secular reach far more penetrating in the conduct of Government than merely to forbid an 'established church.'" Then they turned to "the relevant history of religious education in America," which led them to the conclusion that "Separation in the field of education, then, was not imposed upon unwilling States by force of superior law. In this respect the Fourteenth Amendment merely reflected a principle then dominant in our national life." "Enough has been said," they went on, "to indicate that we are dealing not with a full-blown principle, nor one having the definiteness of a surveyor's metes and bounds. But by 1875 the separation of public education from Church entanglements, of the State from the teaching of religion, was firmly established in the consciousness of the nation." This was the year when President Grant made his speech to the Convention of the Army of the Tennessee on the separation of church and state, and they quoted what Grant said. "By 1894," they continued, "in urging the adoption of such a provision in the New York Constitution, Elihu Root was able to summarize a century of the nation's history: 'It is not a question of religion, or of creed, or of party; it is a question of declaring and maintaining the great American principle of eternal separation between Church and State.'"

The four Justices then turned to the movement for released time.

It was first proposed by a Dr. Wenner in 1905; and, parenthetically, Dr. Wenner's proposal is curiously like Jefferson's views in 1822, which Reed quotes in his dissent. There follow eight pages describing the various permutations of released time, and, again parenthetically, these pages may, I think, be profitably compared with Brandeis' famous factual brief in the Muller case and what the Court there said about it.[37]

Their concurring opinion concludes with Jefferson's metaphor of the wall, Root's phrase, "The great American principle of eternal separation," and a quotation from the best of our contemporary poets, Robert Frost, "Good fences make good neighbors."

Jackson added a further concurring opinion of his own. As candid as ever, Jackson said,

"It is idle to pretend that this task is one for which we can find in the Constitution one word to help us as judges to decide where the secular ends and the sectarian begins in education. Nor can we find guidance in any other legal source. It is a matter on which we can find no law but our own prepossessions."

Reed, though he dissented, approached the problem in exactly the same way. After a demonstration that the Court's decision was very far from what he believed was the intention of either Madison or Jefferson, to his and, let me add, to my satisfaction, Reed turned to "well-recognized and long-established practice," and concluded that "in the light of the meaning given to those words by the precedents, customs, and practices which I have detailed above, I cannot agree with the Court's conclusion . . ." "This Court," he said, "cannot be too cautious in upsetting practices embedded in our society by many years of experience . . . Devotion to the great principle of religious liberty should not lead us into a rigid interpretation of the constitutional guarantee that conflicts with accepted habits of our people."

Thus the Court turned from the intentionally specific language of the First Amendment to the intentionally vague language of the Fourteenth, and then filled its vagueness with what they thought we thought, as expressed by Jefferson in a metaphor, by Grant in a speech following the Civil War, by the political wisdom of a Root, by the insight of a great contemporary poet, and by recent and current educational practice. Frankfurter can be as candid as Jackson. A year later, in a case where several state statutes prohibiting closed

shop contracts were sustained, Frankfurter said that "these are not
matters, like censorship of the press or separation of Church and
State, on which history, through the Constitution, speaks so de-
cisively as to forbid legislative experimentation." [38]

What is decisive, then, on great and critical constitutional issues
is history, and the more recent the better.* So the Constitution be-

---

* When the issue is very great, nothing will do but the present. Nothing
else satisfied the Court in May 1954, in its great decision on racial segregation
in our schools. *Brown* v. *Board of Education,* and *Bolling* v. *Sharpe,* May 17,
1954; 347 U.S. 483, and 497.

Eighty-odd years ago, in 1868, the Fourteenth Amendment imposed on the
States the twin disciplines of due process of law and the equal protection of
the laws. At that time there were few public schools in the South; white children were educated in private schools, and Negro children were scarcely
educated at all. In the North, the vast enterprise of free public schools was
beginning, but there were few Negroes. By the end of the century, the problem
of equal education raised its head. The States tried to deal with it by providing
"separate but equal" schools. The Court took the position in regard to the similar, but far less important, problem of public travel that separate but equal
accommodations were constitutional. In the case of *Plessy* v. *Ferguson,* 163 U.S.
537, in 1896, when it so held, the Court used and approved "separate but
equal" schools as an analogy.

Anyone who now reads the Court's opinion in *Plessy* v. *Ferguson* will find
the Court naïve, if not disingenuous, when it denied that "the enforced
segregation of the two races stamps the colored race with a badge of in-
feriority," and when it said, "If this be so, it is not by reason of anything
found in the act, but solely because the colored race chooses to put that construction on it." Anyone who then gave the problem any serious thought must
have foreseen that, as public education increased, separate schools, if they were
really to be equal, would prove intolerably more expensive than common
schools, and at the same time tempt prejudiced white administrators to make
the colored schools less than equal by spending more than a fair share of the
money appropriated for education on the white schools. This is what happened.
Separate facilities were seldom equal, and where they were not, the Court
told the States that either they must be made so or Negroes could not constitutionally be segregated. The Court did not face the problem whether separate
schools, however equal they might be in respect to buildings, curricula, qualifications and salaries of teachers, etc., were equal in fact.

The Court faced this grave problem in 1954, and said,

"In approaching this problem, we cannot turn the clock back to 1868 when
the Amendment was adopted, or even to 1896 when *Plessy* v. *Ferguson* was
written. We must consider public education in the light of its full development and its present place in American life throughout the Nation. Only in

comes, not a voice, but the trumpet through which we are constantly speaking to a listening Court. Montaigne said, "The laws take their authority from our possession of them and our use of them. It is dangerous to trace them back to their origin. They take on dignity as they roll on, like our rivers. Follow them upstream to their source, it is but a little jet of water that's scarcely discernible, which grows in pride and strength as it grows older. Consider the ancient reasons which gave the start to this famous torrent, full of dignity, honor, and reverence. You will find them so light and so delicate that people here and now who have to weigh everything and reduce it all to reason, and who will take nothing on authority or on credit, it's no marvel if their judgments are often so far removed from the judgments of the people." [39]

Three years later, in 1951, came the case of the released time in the New York public schools.[40] The Illinois schools had released their classrooms as well as time. In New York the religious instruction was given elsewhere. Only school time was released. There was no other relevant difference between the two cases, but six of the justices, including three of the six who had held the released time in Illinois unconstitutional, in the McCollum decision, refused to follow that decision any further, not even far enough to cover the release of school time, without, as in Illinois, the release also of classroom space. They held the New York law constitutional.

The other three justices who had joined in the Illinois decision

---

this way can it be determined if segregation in public schools deprives these plaintiffs of the equal protection of the laws.

"Today, education is perhaps the most important function of state and local governments. Compulsory school attendance laws and the great expenditures for education both demonstrate our recognition of the importance of education to our democratic society. It is required in the performance of our most basic public responsibilities, even service in the armed forces. It is the very foundation of good citizenship. Today it is a principal instrument in awakening the child to cultural values, in preparing him for later professional training, and in helping him to adjust normally to his environment. In these days, it is doubtful that any child may reasonably be expected to succeed in life if he is denied the opportunity of an education. Such an opportunity, where the state has undertaken to provide it, is a right which must be made available to all on equal terms . . .

"We conclude that in the field of public education the doctrine of 'separate but equal' has no place. Separate education facilities are inherently unequal."

and who were still on the bench—unfortunately, Murphy and Rutledge had died—insisted that its principles should have been followed. Jackson said, "The distinction attempted between that case and this is trivial, almost to the point of cynicism . . . Today's judgment will be more interesting to students of psychology and of the judicial processes than to students of constitutional law." Black said that he saw "no significant difference between the invalid Illinois system and that of New York here sustained," and said that he wanted "to reaffirm my faith in the fundamental philosophy expressed in *McCollum* and *Everson* v. *Board of Education.*" Frankfurter agreed with Black "that those principles are disregarded in reaching the result in this case." "Happily," he added, "they are not disavowed by the Court. From this I draw the hope that in future variations of the problem which are bound to come here, these principles may again be honored in the observance."

Now Whitehead gave, as a fourth consequence of the doctrine of law as immanent, that "a reason can now be produced why we should put some limited trust in induction. For if we assume an environment largely composed of a sort of existences whose natures we partly understand, then we have some knowledge of the laws of nature dominating that environment." [41]

"Some limited trust." How much? How far may a court rely upon a principle which it has derived from an immanent order in our law? How far can a decision which it has reached in the immanent order be a precedent for a subsequent decision on a logically similar subject? Or does an immanent law speak only in particulars? Were Black and Frankfurter and Jackson justified in relying on the Illinois decision as a precedent, or should they have started afresh and looked to see if there was an immanent law relating to the release of only school time unaccompanied by the release of a schoolroom?

I suppose my queries resolve, as Whitehead's remark suggests, into the ancient and abiding question of the extent of the validity of inductive reasoning. Logically, but unjustifiably, you could argue that the principles to which these three justices appealed would make the tax exemption of churches equally unconstitutional. President Grant's message to Congress, on which Frankfurter in part relied in the McCollum case, opposed tax exemption as well as direct aid.[42] Why would this reasoning be unjustified? I should say, because another immanent law permitted exemption from taxation. At any rate, I cannot think where else to stop the extension of an immanent law except at the point where another different—I need not say conflicting or even inconsistent—immanent law begins.

Not only tax exemption, but also Bible reading, which is required by statute in a dozen states, Christmas carols and a crèche and the three Wise Men approaching, free lunches, free textbooks, not to speak of the free buses which were held valid in the Everson case,[43] all these "exceptions" make sense, if not logic, as soon as we recognize that we are dealing with an immanent law. These are not quotation, but dubitation marks.

Only "if all the things concerned have the requisite common character," Whitehead says, is exact conformation to an immanent law to be expected. It may be a pity, but I think it is true, that the development of the principles and the philosophy of the McCollum case will stand more securely on the observation and evocation of the presence of other immanent laws than on deductive reasoning. This is not to repudiate reason, but rather to couple it with observation, as the best, I say the only, way toward understanding how we behave as well as how the world behaves around us.

Judges say, in their modesty, that they but find the law. They deny, sometimes with a certain heat, that they make it. Cardozo suggested that they were relying on "the ancient dogma that the law declared by its courts had a Platonic or ideal existence before the act of declaration, in which event the discredited declaration will be viewed as if it had never been, and the reconsidered declaration as law from the beginning.[44] But there is no need of relying on metaphysics. What the courts find is simply the patterns of our immanent law. There is nothing ideal or metaphysical about them. They are factual. They are there to be observed by anyone who will look for them, implicit in our common behavior.

A Reign of Conscience

I am not willing to admit that Learned Hand is ever wrong, but sometimes he can be only half right. He is an eloquent man with a command of rhetoric, and he was seldom more eloquent—few have been—than when he spoke on I Am an American Day, in Central

Park in 1944. He said, "I often wonder whether we do not rest our hopes too much upon constitutions, upon laws and upon courts. These are false hopes; believe me, these are false hopes. Liberty lies in the hearts of men and women; when it dies there, no constitution, no court can save it; no constitution, no law, no court can even do much to help it. While it lies there it needs no constitution, no law, no court to save it. And what is this liberty which must lie in the hearts of men and women? It is not the ruthless, the unbridled will; it is not freedom to do as one likes. That is the denial of liberty, and leads straight to its overthrow. A society in which men recognize no check upon their freedom soon becomes a society where freedom is the possession of only a savage few; as we have learned to our sorrow."[45]

Hand is half right. Though liberty does indeed lie in our hearts, and it is indeed true that if it dies there the Constitution cannot save it, it is not true that our liberties do not need a Bill of Rights.

Madison made the same mistake, at first, when he opposed, or was at least indifferent to, the inclusion of a Bill of Rights in the Constitution. These "parchment barriers" he called it. But then he changed his mind, and agreed with his colleague, Thomas Jefferson, and became the sponsor of the Bill of Rights in the First Congress. Edmond Cahn has told us how Madison changed his mind, and for what reason, right indeed in my opinion.[46] He quotes from a letter Madison wrote to Jefferson on October 17, 1788.

"Wherever the real power in a Government lies, there is the danger of oppression. In our Government the real power lies in the majority of the Community, and the invasion of private rights is *chiefly* to be apprehended, not from acts of Government contrary to the sense of its constituents, but from acts in which the Government is the mere instrument of the major number of the Constituents. This is a truth of great importance, but not yet sufficiently attended to; and is probably more strongly impressed on my mind by facts, and reflections suggested by them, than on yours which has contemplated abuses of power issuing from a very different quarter. Wherever there is an interest and power to do wrong, wrong will generally be done, and not less readily by a powerful and interested party than by a powerful and interested prince.

"What use then may be asked can a bill of rights serve in popular

Governments? I answer the two following which, though less essential than in other Governments, sufficiently recommend the precaution: 1. The Political truths declared in that solemn manner acquire by degrees the character of fundamental maxims of free Government, and as they become incorporated with the national sentiment, counteract the impulses of interest and passion. 2. Altho it be generally true as above stated that the danger of oppression lies in the interested majorities of the people rather than in usurped acts of the Government, yet there may be occasions on which the evil may spring from the latter source; and on such, a bill of rights will be a good ground for an appeal to the sense of the community." [47]

Our hopes do not rest on the Constitution, nor on the law. Our hopes rest on something within us and among us, something which we have made articulate only in part, these "sentiments," to use Madison's words, the liberty in our hearts, to use Hand's. They are false hopes only if they are not evoked and expressed, only when they have not been explained, rationalized, understood, and acknowledged. The courts must carry them across the dark gap between the implicit and the explicit. What we sense but darkly must be said clearly for our salvation.

This, it seems to me, is what our courts do for us. They render into immanent law our political decencies and aspirations. They give us the opportunity to combine a reign of conscience with a republic.

Acknowledgments

Most of the chapter "The Advocate" comes from an article called the "Ethics of Advocacy," which the *Stanford Law Review* published in December 1951.

"The Lawyer" started in an address Harrison Tweed asked me to give to the American Law Institute in St. Louis in September 1949. I spoke it again, at the invitation of Lloyd K. Garrison, in the Association of the Bar of the City of New York, which published it in *The Record* in December 1949. It was then partly rewritten and published by the *Vanderbilt Law Review*, in April 1950. I am indebted to Dean John W. Wade for that. Later, most of it was reprinted in Professor Robert N. Cook, *Legal Drafting* (The Foundation Press, 1951), pp. 104–133. I rewrote it again, at the suggestion of Ralph M. Carson, for the book, *Jurisprudence in Action,* in which the Committee on Post-Admission Legal Education put together a selection of legal essays, published by Baker, Voorhis & Co. in 1953.

The section called "The Trial Court" is in part drawn from another article in the *Vanderbilt Law Review* called "A Modern Supreme Court in a Modern World" (April 1951). It had its origin in an article in the *Pacific Spectator,* "Wringing the Bill of Rights," in the autumn of 1948. I thank Edith Mirrielees for that. I spoke a good deal of it before the Association of American Law Schools in Cincinnati in December 1948. Subsections V, VI, and VII come from another article which the *Stanford Law Review* published in July 1952, called "Ethics in the Law."

Most of "Courts of Appeal" was written for Edmond Cahn's celebration of the sesquicentennial of *Marbury* v. *Madison* at the New York University Law School, Vanderbilt Hall, in February 1953. Professor Cahn presided. Ralph F. Bischoff, John P. Frank, Paul A. Freund, Willard Hurst, and I participated. We each contributed two papers, one long and one short. Some of my long paper came from the article I had written for the *Vanderbilt Law Review,* "A Modern Supreme Court in a Modern World." Then Edmond Cahn wrote an admirable introductory essay and made a book out of it all, *Supreme Court and Supreme Law,* published by the Indiana University Press in 1954.

A good deal of my debt to Professor Willard V. Quine for his wise and sharp explanations of some of the mysteries of modern logic is apparent in these pages. I thank him for all of it, as well as for permission to quote from his book, *From a Logical Point of View*, published by the Harvard University Press.

I am grateful also to the Macmillan Company for permitting me to quote from Whitehead's *Adventures of Ideas* and his *Modes of Thought*, to the Columbia University Press for a long paragraph from Cardozo's *The Paradoxes of Legal Science*, to Cravath, Swaine, and Moore for two quotations from Mr. Swaine's history of *The Cravath Firm*, to Farrar, Straus, and Young, Inc. for paragraphs from Leslie A. White's *The Science of Culture*, to Harper and Brothers for two paragraphs from Aldous Huxley's novel, *After Many a Summer Dies the Swan*, to Houghton Mifflin Company for two paragraphs from Ruth Benedict's *Patterns of Culture* and for Archibald Mac-Leish's verses, to G. P. Putnam's Sons for a paragraph from Gilbert Murray's *The Stoic Philosophy*, and to St Martin's Press for two paragraphs from Dorothy Emmet's *The Nature of Metaphysical Thinking*.

C. P. C.

Notes

THE ADVOCATE

1. Max Radin, "The Permanent Problems of the Law," *Cornell Law Quarterly*, 15:10–11, 1929; and *Law as Logic and Experience* (New Haven: Yale Univ. Press, 1940), pp. 55–56.

2. *Hickman* v. *Taylor*, 329 U.S. 495 at 516.

3. *Panel on "Trial Tactics,"* Section of Insurance Law, American Bar Association (Chicago, 1951), p. 9; and see what Mr. Hocker went on to say, quoted below.

4. Theodore F. T. Plucknett, *A Concise History of the Common Law* (Rochester, N. Y., 1929), pp. 104–105.

5. Charles E. Wyzanski, Jr., "A Trial Judge's Freedom and Responsibility" (Cardozo Lecture for 1952), *The Record*, vol. 7, no. 6, p. 285 (June 1952).

6. Felix Frankfurter, dissenting in *Sacher* v. *United States*, 343 U.S. 1 at 37, 38 (1952).

7. The Hubbard Lectures, May 1914.

8. Elliott E. Cheatham, *Cases and Other Materials on the Legal Profession* (Chicago, 1938), p. 60.

9. Lord Macmillan, *Law and Other Things* (1937), p. 195.

10. Lord Brougham to William Forsyth in 1958, which he put into the third edition of his book, *Hortensius* (London, 1849). Quoted in Cheatham, *Cases and Materials*, p. 227.

11. Canon 15. The Canon quotes George Sharswood, *An Essay on Professional Ethics* (4th ed.; Philadelphia, 1896), pp. 78–79.

12. The case is reported, *Buttle* v. *Saunders*, 2 All England Law Reports 193 (1950), but not the conversations between the Canon and the lawyers, which is unfortunate.

13. Charles P. Curtis, "The Ethics of Advocacy," *Stanford Law Rev.*, December 1951.

14. Some of these proceedings, but not the episode I am telling, can be found in the Matter of Sleeper, 251 Mass. 6 (1925).

15. James E. Harpster, "Christian Advocacy," *Marquette Law Rev.*, vol. 35, p. 414 (1951–1952).

16. Henry S. Drinker, in the *Stanford Law Rev.,* April 1952.

17. Opinion #23.

18. *Holmes-Pollock Letters,* edited by Mark DeWolfe Howe (Cambridge: Harvard Univ. Press, 1946), II, 225–226 (July 2, 12, 1928).

19. Lawrence J. Henderson, "The Practice of Medicine as Applied Sociology," *Transactions of the Association of American Physicians,* li:12 (1936).

20. Samuel Williston, *Life and Law* (Boston: Little, Brown & Co., 1940), p. 271.

21. *Panel on "Trial Tactics,"* Section of Insurance Law, American Bar Association (Chicago, 1951), pp. 9–10.

22. Opinion #287, June 27, 1953. "Opinion of Professional Ethics Committee," *American Bar Association Journal,* 39:985–987 (November 1953).

23. *Ibid.,* p. 986.

24. Williston, *Life and Law,* p. 272.

25. William E. H. Lecky, *The Map of Life, Conduct, and Character* (London, 1899), p. 119. "Honest" is an interesting word to use; he means the "adversary" administration of justice.

26. John Raeburn Green, "The Supreme Court, the Bill of Rights and the States," *Univ. of Pennsylvania Law Rev.,* 97:628–629 (April 1949).

27. Benjamin H. Cardozo, *The Paradoxes of Legal Science* (New York: Columbia Univ. Press, 1928), pp. 59–61; Graham Wallas, *The Art of Thought* (New York, 1926), pp. 119, 96.

28. L. J. Henderson, *Introductory Lectures,* Sociology 23 in Harvard College (2nd ed., October 1938), p. 16. Quoted: Charles P. Curtis, Jr., and Ferris Greenslet, *The Practical Cogitator* (Boston: Houghton Mifflin Co., 1945), p. 258.

29. Benjamin Graham and David L. Dodd, *Security Analysis* (3d ed.; New York: McGraw-Hill, 1951), pp. 666–669.

30. *More Letters of Charles Darwin,* edited by Francis Darwin and A. C. Seward (London, 1903), I, 195.

31. Nieman Reports, Cambridge (April 1950).

32. K. N. Llewellyn, "Book Reviews," *Harvard Law Rev.,* 51:758–759 (1938).

33. Alfred North Whitehead, *Adventures of Ideas* (New York: Macmillan, 1933), p. 213. And on p. 189, "He [Plato] expressly denies omnipotence to his Supreme Craftsman."

34. Louis D. Brandeis, "The Opportunity in the Law," *American Law Rev.,* 39:561 (1905).

35. Including Montaigne in Book 2, ch. 12, translated in Curtis and Greenslet *The Practical Cogitator,* p. 408.

36. Sir Charles John Darling, *Scintillae Juris* (London, 1877), p. 90.

37. Committee on the Bill of Rights, Association of the Bar of the City of New York.

38. James Boswell, *Life of Samuel Johnson* (Hill ed., 1887), II, 47–48.

39. Canon 15, Canons of Professional Ethics of the American Bar Association.

40. *United States* v. *Butler*, 297 U.S. 1 (1936).

41. *Ibid.*, p. 44.

42. Alpheus T. Mason, *Brandeis, A Free Man's Life* (New York: The Viking Press, 1946), p. 506.

43. Robert T. Swaine, *The Cravath Firm* (New York, 1948), II, 9.

44. *Ibid.*, p. 68.

45. *Ibid.*, pp. 45–69.

46. Quoted: Arnold Joseph Toynbee, *A Study of History* (London: Oxford Univ. Press, 1939), vol. 6, pp. 146–147.

47. *Essais de Montaigne* (Charpentier, Variorum ed. 1876), IV, 152 ff. Compare the milder but similar statement of Lecky referred to by Williston.

48. Ralph Waldo Emerson, *Journal*, June 1863.

49. James Gould Cozzens, *Guard of Honor* (New York, 1948), p. 479.

50. T. S. Eliot, *Dante* (London, 1929), pp. 42, 44.

51. Gilbert Murray, *The Stoic Philosophy* (New York: G. P. Putnam's Sons, 1915), p. 50.

52. Ellmann quotes from a letter which he says Yeats probably never sent. Richard Ellmann, *Yeats: The Man and the Masks* (New York: Macmillan, 1948), p. 178.

53. A stanza from some verses by Diogenes J. S. Teufelsdrock, *The Harvard Law School Record*, vol. 8, no. 6, March 16, 1949.

54. Peter Viereck, *Terror and Decorum* (New York: Charles Scribner's Sons, 1948), p. 53.

55. "The Elixir," *The Works of George Herbert* (London, 1846), II, 212,

56. Felix Frankfurter, "Personal Ambitions of Judges," *American Bar Association Journal*, 34:747 (August 1948).

57. Archibald MacLeish, *Collected Poems* (Boston: Houghton Mifflin, 1952), p. 219. There it is in the singular, "question." In its original publication, in 1928, in "The Hamlet of A. MacLeish," it was in the plural "questions."

58. Percy W. Bridgman, *Reflections of a Physicist* (New York: Philosophical Library, 1950), p. 370; see also p. 351.

59. Henderson, *Introductory Lectures*, pp. 15–16.

60. L. J. Henderson, *The Study of Man* (Philadelphia: Univ. of Pennsylvania Press, 1941), p. 3.

61. Plato, the Gorgias, 463B, 465A, and particularly 501A. In his terms, there are three stages, tribe and empeiria, techne, and habitual techne.

62. Irving Babbitt, *On Being Creative* (Boston, 1932), pp. 99–100.

63. Ralph Waldo Emerson, *Essay on Plato*.

64. Goethe, *Zähme Xenien*.

65. Alfred North Whitehead, *Modes of Thought* (New York: The Macmillan Company, 1949), pp. 5, 11, 12. Quoted by Dorothy M. Emmet, *The Nature of Metaphysical Thinking* (New York: St Martin's Press, 1949), p. 195. (Published in England by Macmillan & Co., Ltd., London.)

66. *Writings of Henry David Thoreau* (Boston, 1906), vol. 7, p. 289; in his journal on November 30, 1841.

THE LAWYER

1. Mark DeWolfe Howe, "Book Reviews," *Harvard Law Rev.*, 60:842 (1947).

2. Oliver Wendell Holmes, *Collected Legal Papers* (New York: Harcourt, Brace, and Howe, 1920), p. 208.

3. Anton-Hermann Chroust, *Harvard Law Rev.*, 58:573 ff. (April, 1945).

4. Swaine, *The Cravath Firm*, II, 465.

5. James Bradley Thayer, *A Preliminary Treatise on Evidence* (Boston, 1898), p. 405.

6. F. Vaughan Hawkins, "On the Principles of Legal Interpretation" quoted in Thayer, *Preliminary Treatise*, Appendix C, pp. 580–581.

7. *Restatement of Property*, Vol. III, sec. 241, Comment (c).

8. Scott on Trusts, sec. 164.1 (Little, Brown & Co.).

9. Wigmore, Sec. 2461.

10. Thayer, *Preliminary Treatise*, p. 428.

11. *Throckmerton v. Tracy*, Plowden, 160; quoted by Wigmore in sec. 2461.

12. *Doe v. Dring*, 2 M. & S. 448 at 454 (1814).

13. *Doe v. Gwillim*, 5 B. and Ad. 122 at 129 (1833); also quoted by Wigmore, sec. 2461, sec. 2459.

14. Wigmore, sec. 2461.

15. *Mahoney v. Grainger*, 283 Mass. 189.

16. See note 6.

17. *Scott on Trusts*, sec. 164.1.

18. John Chipman Gray, *The Nature and Sources of the Law* (2nd ed.; New York: Macmillan, 1927), pp. 172–173.

19. "How Far Is a Judge Free in Rendering a Decision?," a radio broadcast in 1933, published by the University of Chicago Press, reprinted in *The Spirit of Liberty*, edited by Irving Dilliard (New York: Knopf, 1953), p. 106.

20. *United States v. Klinger*, 199 Fed. 2d 645 at 648.

21. December 6, 1948; 335 U.S. 377.

22. G. L. ch. 234, sec. 1.

23. *Commonwealth v. Welosky*, 276 Mass. 398 (1930).

24. *The Record*, June, 1947, p. 227. And from the bench in *Shapiro v. United States*, 335 U.S. 1, when the Court was construing the Emergency Price Control Act.

25. Robert H. Jackson, "The Meaning of Statutes," *American Bar Association Journal*, 34:535 (July 1948). And from the bench, in *Schwegmann Bros. v. Calvert Corp.*, 341 U.S. 384 at 395–396.

26. 18 U.S. Code Section 3486.

27. *Adams v. Maryland*, 347 U.S. 179 at 183.

28. In an article on The Labor Management Relations Act, *Harvard Law Rev.*, 61:45 (November, 1947).

29. Mason, *Brandeis*, p. 579 n.

30. *Spector Motor Service v. Walsh*, 139 Fed. 2d 809 at 823.

31. *United States* v. *Schwimmer*, 279 U.S. 644; *United States* v. *Macintosh*, 283 U.S. 605; *United States* v. *Bland*, 283 U.S. 636.

32. *United States* v. *Girouard*, 149 Fed. 2d 760 at 767; 328 U.S. 61; 1946. Another similar case is Judge John J. Parker's decision in the Barnette case over the flag salute in schools, 47 Fed. Supp. 251, when the Supreme Court reversed the Gobitis decision in 322 U.S. 292.

33. *Williston on Contracts,* sec. 603 (Baker, Voorhis & Co.).

34. *Ibid.,* secs. 604, 607.

35. Holmes, *Collected Legal Papers,* pp. 203–204; and *Harvard Law Rev.,* 12:417 (1899).

36. Willard Van Orman Quine, *Methods of Logic* (New York: Henry Holt & Co., 1950), pp. 203–208.

37. MacLeish, "America was Promises," *Collected Poems,* p. 341.

38. *Juridical Society Papers* (London, 1863), II, 298.

39. W. Stanley Jevons, *Elementary Lessons in Logic* (New York, 1895), Lesson V.

40. Clarence Irving Lewis, *Analysis of Knowledge and Valuation* (La Salle, Ind.: Open Court, 1947), p. 39.

41. Max Radin, for one, is an exception. In "Statutory Interpretation," *Harvard Law Rev.,* 43:863–885 (April 1930), he uses the terms, a determinable and a determinate, for which he refers to W. E. Johnson, *Logic* (1921). A statute is a determinable, and a determinate its application, as I understand it.

42. Alan Gardiner, *Speech and Language* (Oxford, 1932), pp. 20, 19.

43. Holmes, *Collected Legal Papers,* p. 209.

44. Dissenting in *New England Trust Company* v. *Eaton*, 140 Mass. 532 at 548.

45. See note 2.

46. Quine, *Methods of Logic,* p. 197.

47. *In re* Jackson, 1933 Chancery 237.

48. O. W. Holmes, *The Common Law* (Boston: Little, Brown & Co., 1881), p. 309; *Raffles* v. *Wichelhaus,* 2 H & C 906.

49. Holmes, *Collected Legal Papers,* p. 205.

50. *National Mutual Insurance Co.* v. *Tidewater Transfer Co.,* 337 U.S. 582 (1949). Charles Bunn, *A Brief Survey of the Jurisdiction and Practice of the Courts of the United States* (5th ed.; St. Paul: West Publishing Co., 1949), pp. 47–49.

51. Thomas Hobbes, *The Leviathan* (Everyman's Library Ed., ed. by Ernest Rhys, New York: E. P. Dutton), Part 2, p. 193.

52. Arthur Koestler, *Insight and Outlook* (New York: The Macmillan Co., 1949), pp. 310, 318, 412.

53. *Ibid.,* p. 413.

54. Aldous Huxley, *After Many A Summer Dies the Swan* (New York: Harper & Brothers, 1939), pp. 179–180.

55. Quoted by J. Mitchell Morse, *New York Herald-Tribune's* book section, May 1, 1949.

56. Goethe, *Maxims and Reflections.* Günther Müller's Ger. ed. (Stuttgart: Alfred Kröner, 1949), #596.

57. Learned Hand, "Thou Shalt Not Ration Justice," *Brief Case* (April, 1951), vol. IX, no. 4, pp. 4–5.

58. Edmund Wilson, *The Triple Thinkers* (New York: Oxford Univ. Press, 1948), p. ix.

59. Pascal, *Pensées,* #64 (Paris, 1922), p. 345.

60. *Holmes-Laski Letters,* edited by Mark DeWolfe Howe (Cambridge: Harvard Univ. Press, 1953), I, 605 (March 28, 1924).

61. *Time,* December 12, 1949, pp. 36–37.

62. Montaigne, Book I, ch. 24.

63. Heading to chapter IX in Andre Maurois, *A La Recherche de Marcel Proust* (Paris: Hachette, 1949).

64. Kant, *Critique of Pure Reason* (trans. by N. K. Smith; London, 1929), p. 310. Quoted by Ernst Cassirer, *An Essay on Man* (Anchor ed.; Garden City, Doubleday & Co., 1953), p. 228.

65. William Empson, *Seven Types of Ambiguity* (2nd ed.; New Directions, 1949), pp. 242–243.

66. Huxley, *After Many a Summer,* p. 77.

67. In this chapter my debt to John Dewey's *Art as Experience* is obvious.

THE TRIAL COURT

1. *Holmes-Laski Letters*, I, 385, 723; and Holmes, *Uncollected Papers,* edited by Harry C. Shriver (New York: Central Book Co., 1936), p. 178.

2. *The Spirit of Liberty,* pp. 62–63.

3. Goethe, March 30, 1831.

4. Bertrand Russell, *Human Knowledge* (New York: Simon & Schuster, 1948), p. 423.

5. This is what Holmes said in the course of his great dissent in the Lochner case. *Lochner* v. *New York*, 198 US. 76 (1905).

6. *Chicago B. & Q. Ry.* v. *Babcock,* 204 U.S. 585, 598 (1907).

7. Joseph H. Beale, *Conflict of Laws* (New York, 1916), sec. 118.

8. *The Spirit of Liberty,* "Is A Judge Free," pp. 105–106.

9. Restatement, Torts, sec. 559 (1938).

10. Lord Goddard, in *Laski* v. *Newark Advertiser,* quoting from *The King* v. *Cuthell*, 27 How. St. Tr. 642, 675 (1799). The transcript of the trial was published by the *London Daily Express*, in 1946.

11. *United States* v. *Levine*, 83 Fed. 2d 156, 157 (2d Cir. 1936).

12. Holmes, *The Common Law,* p. 123.

13. Pascal, *Pensées,* No. 1. Pascal's *Pensées* are the short notes and memoranda, written on bits of paper or briefly dictated, which he made for the book he did not live to write, Brunschicg sorted them out and put this one at the beginning.

14. Francis W. Peabody, "The Care of the Patient," *Doctor and Patient* (New York: The Macmillan Co., 1930), p. 27.

15. See below.

16. Emmet, *Metaphysical Thinking*, p. 141.

17. This is but a glimpse of what the jurists are calling the parental function of the law, which is a dominant concern of Soviet law. See Harold J. Berman, *Justice in Russia* (Cambridge: Harvard Univ. Press, 1950) and K. N. Llewellyn's Lectures on Jurisprudence, which are mimeographed for his classes.

18. Wyzanski, "A Trial Judge's Freedom," p. 288.

19. In these cases Justice Bernard L. Shientag of the Supreme Court of New York, who was himself one of those judges, considered juries essential.

20. Salvador de Madariaga, *Don Quixote, An Introductory Essay in Psychology* (London, Oxford Univ. Press, 1935), p. 105.

21. Oliver Wendell Holmes, *Elsie Venner* (Boston, 1888), p. 47.

22. John Woodcock, "Note Taking by Jurors," *Dickinson Law Rev.*, 55:335 (1951). Mr. Woodcock justly points out that when some jurors were illiterate, to take notes would be the privilege of a few, but that is not the point I have in mind.

23. *Cheek* v. *State*, 35 Indiana Reports 492 at 495 (1871).

24. "Should Jurors Be Allowed to Take Notes?" *J. Am. Jud. Soc'y*, 32:57 (1948).

25. L. L. Bomberger, "Jurors Should Be Allowed to Take Notes," *J. Am. Jud. Soc'y*, 32:57–58 (1948).

26. Phil M. McNagny, "Jurors Should Not Be Allowed to Take Notes," *J. Am. Jud. Soc'y*, 32:58, 59 (1948).

27. Emmet, *Metaphysical Thinking*, p. 142.

28. Clyde Kluckhohn and Dorothea Leighton, *The Navaho* (Cambridge: Harvard Univ. Press, 1948), pp. 103, 71.

29. Published by the *London Daily Express*, 367 (1946).

30. O. W. Holmes, "Book Notices," 5 *Am. Law Rev.*, 5:540 (1871), Holmes, *Uncollected Papers*, p. 90.

31. O. W. Holmes, "Codes and the Arrangement of the Law," *Am. Law Rev.*, 5:1 (1870); Holmes, *Uncollected Papers*, p. 63.

32. Harold J. Berman, "The Challenge of Soviet Law," 62 *Harvard Law Rev.*, 220, 449–451 (1949); Berman, *Justice in Russia*, p. 201.

33. Sterling Dow discovered and explained the elaborations of this system in 1939. *Harvard Studies in Classical Philology* (Cambridge: Harvard Univ. Press, 1951), L, 81 ff.

34. 332 U.S. 261 (1947). Also *Moore* v. *New York*, 333 U.S. 565, (1948); and what Learned Hand said in the case of the Communists, *United States* v. *Dennis*, 183 Fed. 2d 201, 216–24 (2d Cir. 1950).

35. 332 U.S. at 299–300.

36. Professor Jerome Michael of Columbia University. Judge Samuel C. Coleman presided. Ass'n Bar of City of New York, *The Record*, vol. 5, no. 4, pp. 199–200 (1950).

37. Holmes, *Collected Legal Papers*, pp, 237–238.

38. Radin, *Law as Logic and Experience*, p. 18.

39. 1 Coke's *Institutes*, sec. 138.
40. Whitehead, *Adventures of Ideas*, p. 374.
41. *Ibid.*, p. 185.
42. Alfred Jules Ayer, *Language, Truth and Logic* (London: Victor Gollancz, 1950), p. 107.
43. Restatement of Torts, sec. 12 (1934). And see too the compliment which the Restatement of Trusts pays the superior trustee, "On the other hand, if the trustee has a greater degree of skill than that of a man of ordinary intelligence, he is liable for a loss resulting from the failure to use such skill as he has." Sec. 227, comment (c) on clause (a).
44. *Collected Papers of Charles S. Pierce* (Cambridge: Harvard Univ. Press, 1931) I, 56.
45. Pascal, *Pensées* No. 465, p. 546.
46. A. J. Ayer, "On the Analysis of Moral Judgements," *Horizon*, XX:176 (September 1949).
47. Ruth Benedict, *The Chrysanthemum and the Sword* (Boston: Houghton Mifflin, 1946), pp. 222 ff. E. R. Dodds, *The Greeks and the Irrational* (Berkeley: Univ. of California Press, 1951), pp. 17, 26, claims that the society described by Homer was a shame-culture and says we are now moving out of a guilt-culture.
48. *Holmes-Pollock Letters*, II, 3; *Holmes-Laski Letters*, II, 1183.
49. *Jordan* v. *De George*, 341 U.S. 223, 232 (1951) (dissenting opinion).
50. *Repouille* v. *United States*, 165 Fed. 2d 152 (2d Cir. 1947).
51. Röpke keeps using the simile of humus. Röpke, *The Social Crisis of Our Time* (1950).
52. Ruth Benedict, *Patterns of Culture* (Boston: Houghton Mifflin, 1934), pp. 2–3.
53. *Ibid.*, pp. 252–253.
54. John Selden, *Table-talk* (London, 1689), p. 104.
55. Whitehead, *Science and the Modern World* (Pelican ed.; Penguin Books Ltd., 1938), p. 15.
56. Clyde Kluckhohn, *Mirror for Man* (New York: Whittlesey House, 1949), p. 36.
57. Edmond Cahn, *The Sense of Injustice* (New York Univ. and Oxford Univ. Press, 1949), p. 121.
58. Emerson, *Journal*, June 22, 1843.
59. Henry David Thoreau, Walden (Modern Library ed; New York, 1947), p. 646.
60. G. E. Fasnacht, *Acton's Political Philosophy* (London: Hollis and Carter, 1952), p. 32n.
61. *The Philosophy of Peirce*, edited by Justus Buchler (New York: Harcourt, Brace, 1940), p. 47.
62. Leslie A. White, *The Science of Culture* (New York: Farrar, Straus & Young, Inc., 1949), pp. 156–158.
63. Galatians 2:21. Let me say that the word "righteousness" in both the Greek and the Latin is justice.

COURTS OF APPEAL

1. For example, Rule 52 of the Federal Rules of Civil Procedure.
2. *United States* v. *Aluminum Co. of America*, 148 Fed. 2d 416 at 433 (2d Cir. 1945). You can read what the Supreme Court has said about the complicated character of a "finding of fact" and its reluctance, and yet readiness, to review and reverse one that lay "close to opinion regarding the whole nature of our government and the duties and immunities of citizenship" in *Baumgartner* v. *United States*, 322 U.S. 665 at 670 (1944).
3. C. P. Curtis, Jr., "Due, and Democratic, Process of Law," *Wisconsin Law Rev.*, March 1944.
4. MacLeish, *Collected Poems*, p. 173.
5. Charles G. Haines, *The American Doctrine of Judicial Supremacy* (New York, 1914), p. 288; quoted by Brandeis at the end of his dissent in *Eisner* v. *Macomber*, 252 U.S. 189 at 238 (1920).
6. 337 U.S. 582 at 654.
7. Shakespeare, *The Tempest*, Act II, scene 1.
8. Willard Van Orman Quine, "Two Dogmas of Empiricism," *The Philosophical Rev.*, January 1951; and *From a Logical Point of View* (Cambridge: Harvard Univ. Press, 1953), p. 22.
9. Bertrand Russell, *A History of Western Philosophy* (New York: Simon and Schuster, 1945), pp. 165, 200.
10. 252 U.S. 189 (1920) at 207, 208, 211, 219.
11. I am grateful to Professor Quine for the paragraph I have quoted, and recurrently for his clear counsel. If you read on in Quine, you will find that he does not approve of leaving any remnant of Aristotelian essentialism in the notion of meaning.
12. 10 Wheaton 428 (1825).
13. *Waring et al.* v. *Clarke*, 5 Howard 441 (1847).
14. *The Genesee Chief et al.* v. *Fitzhugh et al.*, 12 Howard 443 at 457 (1851).
15. *United States* v. *Lovett*, 328 U.S. 303 at 321.
16. *United States* v. *Underwriters Association*, 322 U.S. 533.
17. *Paul* v. *Virginia*, 8 Wallace 168; *Hooper* v. *California*, 155 U.S. at 648; *New York Life Insurance Company* v. *Deer Lodge County*, 231 U.S. at 495.
18. 321 U.S. 649 at 665. This is a quotation from Brandeis' dissent in *Burnet* v. *Coronado Oil & Gas Co.*, 285 U.S. 393 at 410, as the Court recognized.
19. *Ashwander* v. *Tennessee Valley Authority*, 297 U.S. 288, 346–48 (1936).
20. Charles Fairman, *American Constitutional Decisions* (rev. ed.; New York: Henry Holt & Co., 1950), p. 392.
21. United Press, July 16, 1948; *New York Times*, July 17, 1948, p. 6.
22. *Oyama* v. *California*, 332 U.S. 633, 663 (1948).
23. *American Communications Ass'n* v. *Douds*, 339 U.S. 382, 419 (1950).
24. *MacDougall* v. *Green*, 335 U.S. 281, 283–284 (1948).

25. *Ibid.*, 289–290.
26. H. R. Doc. 264, 78th Cong. 1st Sess. 1 (1943).
27. *Lovett v. United States*, 66 Fed. Supp. 142, 144 (1945).
28. 89 *Cong. Rec.* 4482–87, 4546–56, 4581–4605 (House), 5023–24 (Senate) (1943). The *Washington Post*, as usual, was more than well aware of what was going on. Herbert Elliston's editorial is reprinted in 89 *Cong. Rec.* 4548 (1943).
29. *United States v. Lovett*, 328 U.S. 303, 316–318 (1946).
30. *Ibid.*, 318–319, 321.
31. Article III, sec. 2. (Italics mine.)
32. *Ex parte* McCardle, 7 Wallace 506, 1869. Charles Fairman, *Mr. Justice Miller and the Supreme Court* (Cambridge: Harvard Univ. Press, 1938), ch. 6.
33. Article III, sec. 1.
34. Reed quotes this from Madison, 333 U.S. at 244, but not Sylvester, which you will find in the records of the First Congress. 1 *Annals of Congress* 730 (1789).
35. 333 U.S. 203 (1948).
36. Louisa Clark, "Book Reviews," *Harvard Law Rev.*, 63:731 (1950).
37. *Muller v. Oregon*, 208 U.S. 412 at 420 (1908).
38. *American Federation of Labor v. American Sash Co.*, 335 U.S. 538 at 550 (1949).
39. Montaigne, *The Apology for Raymond Sebond*, Essays, Bk. 2, ch. 12.
40. *Zorach v. Clauson*, 343 U.S. 306.
41. Whitehead, *Adventures of Ideas*, p. 143.
42. See Rutledge's dissent in the Everson case, 330 U.S. 1, at 63–74 (1947), and Arthur E. Sutherland, "Due Process and Disestablishment," *Harvard Law Rev.*, 62:1337–8 (1949).
43. 330 U.S. 1.
44. *Great Northern Ry. v. Sunburst Co.*, 287 U.S. 358 at 365 (1932).
45. *The Spirit of Liberty*, pp. 189–190.
46. Edmond N. Cahn, "Madison and the Pursuit of Happiness," *New York Univ. Law Rev.*, 27:265, 276 (April 1952).
47. *The Writings of James Madison* (Gaillard Hunt, ed.; 1904), pp. 269, 272–273. The Oxford Dictionary gives as one of the definitions of *sentiment:* "6. What one feels with regard to something; mental attitude (of approval or disapproval, etc.); an opinion or view as to what is right or agreeable. Often pl. with collective sense."

Index